A Hundred *More* Things Japanese

A Hundred *More* Things Japanese

Japan Culture Institute

Edited by Murakami Hyoe and Donald Richie
First printing, 1980
Published by the Japan Culture Institute
201 Park Avenue, 20, Sendagaya 1-chome, Shibuya-ku, Tokyo 151
Printed by the Toppan Printing Co., Ltd.
Distributor: Japan Publications Trading Co., Ltd.
P.O. Box 5030 Tokyo International, Tokyo 101-31, Japan

ISBN 0-87040-472-5
Printed in Japan

Foreword

The assembling of the first one hundred things Japanese in 1975 exhausted the possibilities neither of Japan itself nor of the many readers whose enthusiasm has made us feel that now, five years later, this second hundred things Japanese might be welcomed.

The idea of introducing this material—various objects and concepts—as separate "things" has the advantage of presenting the context, Japan itself, in a relatively new light. Sensibility becomes fairly deadened when one knows that, say, Fujisan will appear in the all too familiar context of geisha and cherry blossoms. But here, as a look at the table of contents will indicate, Mount Fuji is in the surprising but (as a moment's consideration will ascertain) much more fitting company of naked festivals on one hand and the Japanese concepts of water on the other.

The ordering of this book, then, offers one image after the other, but each is in a novel and telling alignment with its neighbor. One result of this is, we have found, the freshness that only a new context can give. And here, perhaps, the foreign reader may also receive a new insight into his own "things."

Again, as in the previous collection, we have asked only foreigners to write about Japan. Here, too, our aim was freshness. We had seen in the first book that the angles from which foreigners in this country view our "things" often rid them of the sometimes deadening associations that they must have for us Japanese. The eyes of foreigners gave us a new way of looking at ourselves. And we believe that this view—one that takes nothing for granted—is, again, the one we should share with our foreign readers.

As we mentioned in the first volume, we think that viewing a living country through a mosaic of one hundred things is neither impractical nor quixotic. Rather, we feel that this may be the way to present a vital and evolving culture. Viewing things from a new angle and from within a new context is, indeed, the only way, perhaps, to ensure vitality and to suggest complexity.

Any book is a collaborative effort, and this one being no exception the editors of the Japan Culture Institute wish to express their appreciation to all whose cooperation has made the book possible. Special thanks to Clifton Karhu for the illustrations; to Aoki Shinji, Aoyama Fujio, Fujitsuka Haruo, Fukasawa Tatsuji, Futamura Jirō, Igarashi Senhiko, Iwasaki Yūko, Kume Shigeru, and Sakakibara Kazuo for their photographs; and to the Ministry of Posts and Telecommunications, Defense Agency, Metropolitan Police Department, National Theater, Shōgakukan, Japan Travel Bureau, the Mainichi Newspapers, Sankei Shimbun, TV Asahi, Sōtō Zen Buddhist Sect, Franell Gallery, Theater Mingei, and Seibu Department Store for furnishing photographs.

December, 1979
Tokyo

Editors' Note

Japanese words in this book are spelled according to the modified Hepburn system and are printed in italics the first time they appear in the essays, except for those words that have entered the English vocabulary and are listed in *Webster's New World Dictionary* (Second College Edition). Japanese names are printed in the Japanese order, family name first.

A list of the historical periods of Japan mentioned in the essays appears on page 212.

Fujisan, 富士山

Mount Fuji (*san* here means "mountain").

When visitors ask me where to catch Japanese people at their most characteristic, I usually suggest, "Climb Fujisan with them." I have made the climb a dozen times myself—in spite of the Japanese proverb that only a fool climbs Fuji more than once. But, to quote our own William Blake: a fool who persists in his folly becomes wise. Fujisan has taught many of us a great deal about Japan.

I will sing the praises
Of this exalted peak
As long as I have breath.

Thus wrote the eighth-century poet Yamabe no Akahito, accurately summarizing the way Japanese still feel about Mount Fuji twelve centuries later. Even the commercialization of the name by a major bank, a brand of ice cream, a maker of ball bearings, a chain of bowling alleys, and a host of other enterprises has not altered this sentiment.

The mountain itself—which measures 3,776 meters if you don't count the radar antenna—was already there, quietly smoking away, when the first Japanese arrived from the island of Kyushu. The name itself is said to come from the verb "to burst forth" in the language of the Ainu. Those former inhabitants of the islands probably witnessed the eruption that formed Fuji's perfect outer cone in a single week of belching fire and raining lava some twenty thousand years ago—the wind from the west giving it its ever so slight tilt toward the sea.

The Japanese pioneers affixed the name of one of their goddesses, Konohanasakuya-hime, to the mountain. She is a relative of the Sun Goddess, and so an ancestor of all the Japanese people, with strong connections to the imperial family and (because you can see it so clearly from the summit) the rising sun. Fuji, combining strength, calm, and beauty, thus offers the perfect patriotic package, and the basic motivation of the two million Japanese (plus a few foreigners) who climb at least part-way up every year.

The last five thousand feet or so is an immense cone of cinders without a tree or a blade of grass. There are, in this section, five "stations," clusters of stone huts where you can lie on a straw mat for a few hours or refresh yourself with tea or noodles, at prices that grow steeper with the mountain. Day and night there is a constant double file of humanity winding up and down the trail, chanting invocations to the goddess of the mountain, telling jokes, and singing pop songs. But the word you hear more than any other is *"ganbatte"*—"press on!"—the word the Japanese use to encourage one another to persevere.

Surprisingly, most of the summer climbers make it to the top, where a row of souvenir shops and shrines, and even a tiny post office, awaits them. The trail worn by millions of feet, the simple and democratic accommodations, and the cheerful determination of the crowds are as agelessly Japanese as a woodblock by Hiroshige. But there is only one way really to understand the meaning of Mount Fuji, and that is to climb it. *Ganbatte!*

Murray Sayle

Hadaka-matsuri, はだか祭

Naked festivals.

Annual festivals in which the participants are fully or partially naked are still found in many places in Japan. Such public nudity in a land noted for official prudery is perhaps to be explained in that bodily modesty is of fairly recent origin but the urge to nudity is ancient.

Specifically, this urge is religious and has its roots in both Shinto, Japan's first organized religion, and, say some scholars, whatever atavistic religion preceded it. There are, in the event, few Buddhist naked festivals—and certainly no Christian ones. Rather, the various forms that these festivals take are so Shinto-based that the most casual visitor to any shrine partakes of them.

A major ritual is that of purification. Undergone, the rite cleanses: one is as though reborn. An ancient belief is that the naked man is again a child; washed of his impurities, he is again unsullied as a child. Then, like the baby, he is washed. Many naked festivals conclude with mass lustrations—usually in rivers, lakes, or the sea.

The visitor to the ordinary shrine partakes of this same impulse when he washes his hands and rinses his mouth. The religious observation is identical, the difference is only in degree. Also, most shrines receive the majority of their visitors on New Year's. Naked festivals usually occur in January or February. The new year is in both instances a propitious time to become new oneself.

A visitor to any shrine notices the many talismans and may even acquire some. Here also a parallel is found in the naked festival. Hundreds of nude men struggle to obtain good-luck charms. Or, conversely, one of their number is made scapegoat and the hundreds struggle to touch him and pass on their yearly accumulation of bad luck. A manifestation of the same thing is seen in the ordinary shrine where people tie bad-fortune slips to eaves or branches and leave them there.

All Shinto shrines provide oracles—usually in the form of divination rods—and in the naked festival oracular divination is also observed. Here it usually takes the form of competitions—races, wrestling, tugs of war—to determine divine will.

Finally (though there are many other similarities as well), there is the showing of sacred objects. In the everyday shrine these are displayed or, occasionally, carried about during religious observances. In the naked festivals this becomes an elaborate procession—the most famous of which is the mass carrying of the *o-mikoshi* portable shrine.

Thus, ordinary Shinto observances (as well as some even earlier, usually having to do with propitiation and fertility) form the base of Japan's naked festivals—evidence of a continuing and deeply felt religious impulse.

Donald Richie

Chadō, 茶道

The tea ceremony, also called *sadō*.

In some of its most distinctively Japanese aspects, the celebrated tea ceremony shares things in common with the equally celebrated Western classical ballet. Both are highly prescribed by elaborate rules and regulations, both are intolerable unless the rules and regulations are scrupulously observed, and both are hopelessly boring if nothing is added to the meticulous observation of the rules and regulations. This is where the resemblance

stops. The pleasures derived from the two are of different genres. In ballet, dancers perform for the enjoyment of a physically passive, mentally observant audience; whereas, in the tea ceremony, everyone performs to an extent, and the greater the participation, the greater the pleasure.

As all manuals on the subject set forth in abundant detail, in its basic form, the tea ceremony is a ritualized way of preparing and offering to guests a beverage made of finely powdered green tea and hot water. The manuals further tell how, in the late fifteenth century, a number of tea masters rejected the luxury and display associated by wealthy lords with preparation and consumption of this drink and developed what is called the tea of refined simplicity. These tea masters, the most famous of whom was Sen no Rikyū (1521–91), insisted that the tea ceremony be performed in small, or very small, rooms and that bamboo and other humble materials replace the ivories and rich substances ostentatious lords had loved to use. They deemphasized imported Chinese and Korean wares and, by using bowls and vessels made at home, stimulated an important aspect of the Japanese art of ceramics.

Gradually they succeeded in evolving an art form in which both host and guests perform in ways demanding knowledge of poetry, painting, classical literature, flower arrangement, various crafts, and hospitality. Their tea ceremony existed in a microcosm where money (ostensibly) did not matter, class was not considered, and discernment and elaborate courtesy counted most.

Much time has passed since then. The tea ceremony has survived and is probably more popular today than at any other time in its history. In fact, for some, it is a big business meeting the needs of the many polite young ladies who consider it an essential accomplishment, rather as playing the piano and watercolor painting were for nice girls of the age of Victoria.

The tea ceremony is, of course, much more than an accomplishment. It is a vital part of general Japanese culture because of its encyclopedic inclusiveness. To become truly adept at it, a person must study for a lifetime and even then will never master all there is to know. The tea ceremony is an education from which there can be no graduation.

Richard L. Gage

Mizu, 水
Water.

The legend of Urashima Tarō tells of a young fisherman who spent a year under the sea, only to find upon his return that he had been gone a century.

Several of the images in this story suggest interesting and perhaps unique views of water. I remember that when I heard Japanese water for the first time—the rhythmic clacking of the water mortar—I thought of time. The seconds and minutes seemed to be ticked off, a kind of water clock that no one used to tell time. Then I realized that time, like water, is also fluid. In spring when the waters run higher and faster the mortar would beat more quickly; in the frozen winter, slowly or not at all. This, I realized, is the real pulse of nature—the flow of water.

Another image in the legend suggests that water preserves

youth. There is in Japan ample evidence that it does. Every village seems to have its spring or its well, and they all have healing and rejuvenating powers. One such is the *wakasai* (roughly, "well of youth") at Nara, where in the coldest days of winter the priests of Tōdai-ji gather to draw water in the ritual called *omizutori*. This water is also believed to offer health and youth. In the old days, from this and other wells, the first water drawn on New Year's morning was *wakamizu*, or the "water of youth."

One's most vivid memories of Japan are often linked with water: the flooded springtime paddies, the running rivulets along every road, the many ponds and pools. To gauge the importance of water to Japan one need remember not only the cultivation of rice, but also the many parts of Japanese culture dependent upon water: *ikebana* (flower arranging), the tea ceremony, landscape gardening, cloth dyeing, and much of the poetry, including the famous Bashō haiku about the frog jumping into the ancient pond.

The imagery of water permeates Japan. Listen to the language: *mizu ga hairu* ("water coming in") means, in the old language, to have a rest; *mizu irazu* ("no water between us") means to be among ourselves, with no outsiders; *mizu ni nagasu* ("to flow with the water") means to forgive and forget.

All of these (and many more) water-based phrases smooth and soften contemporary life. They are like the little fountains one often finds in the severe contemporary concrete buildings. Perhaps it is this soft, inner rhythm of water that has given the Japanese culture its dominant characteristics: the ability to let go and to flow, the assumption of fluidity, the haziness and even the vagueness, the naturalness.

Anthony V. Liman

Tsumikusa, 摘草

Herb gathering.

The techniques of landscape painting Japan learned from the Chinese, but already by the eleventh century the Japanese were creating richly colorful landscapes with mineral pigments, guided by a perceptibly Japanese sensibility and by Shinto tastes. Reproductions in books fail to convey the directness of these hues. I was certainly shocked the first time I saw the mineral pigment *rokushō* in a real painting. It was such an audaciously unmuted *green* green. Colors like that were not supposed to exist in subtle, misty Japan.

And then one April a friend took me deep into the mountains to spend several days welcoming spring, working on a joint translation project, and gathering *warabi,* or bracken fern, shoots. There, intensified by the newly warm moisture exuding from the earth, was the same pure rokushō—no longer blatantly intrusive but vibrant in the tips of pine needles, exuberant tree buds, and the limitless wild grasses.

All tensions accumulated from a winter of city living evaporated as she and I reveled in the activity of reaching for another and another and another of the lovely green things just lifting their furls for the first time. Aside from bird and wind noises, the only sound was the gentle snap-snap as our fingers cleanly broke the fresh shoots. At first they seemed quite few and far between, but as my eyes gradually accustomed themselves to distinguishing one quality of green from another, they appeared in ever increasing abundance. Those evenings our vegetarian suppers more than made up in succulence what they lacked in variety.

Although that experience had all the satisfying qualities of a spring rite, I had no idea at the time with what great garlands of tradition it was strung. The Japanese have always loved to turn seasonal forays into formal occasions—witness the cherry-blossom-viewing parties attended yearly by thousands. Since early times seasonal greens have been gathered formally on several occasions during the year. Everyone from imperial courtiers to mountain peasants collected the "seven grasses of spring," *haru no nanakusa,* during the first few days of the New Year and ate them cooked with soft rice. (On the lunar calendar, New Year's Day fell near the beginning of our February.) And then, in the late third or early fourth month of the year the bursting advent of spring was celebrated with *tsumikusa,* "picking greens."

Unlike the nanakusa, the tsumikusa greens were not specified but varied from place to place, so we were completely in tune with the best of Japanese tradition there in the mountains, seeking out the delicious specialties of the region, experimenting with ways to bring out their natural taste—and enjoying to the fullest the seasonal green.

Sharon Ann Rhoads

Hanagoyomi, 花暦

A kind of almanac (literally, "flower calendar").

"How do you do *ikebana* in the winter when there are no flowers?" someone asked me during a demonstration I was giving for some friends on a recent trip to California. It is natural enough to think: flowers bloom only in spring; no flowers, no flower arranging. But it is, in fact, wrong on two counts.

First, shortly after I had begun ikebana in Japan, I found it to be an art form that relied as much on branches, leaves, and grasses as on flowers—perhaps even more so. Also, nowadays, plants may be dispensed with altogether in favor of metal, glass, ceramics, or just about anything that suits the fancy.

Second, flowers don't belong to spring, or to any season for

that matter. Once one's expectations have been adjusted accordingly, winter in Japan can come to mean narcissus breaking through the cold earth, bright red camellias with their sharp, lustrous green leaves against the snow, not to mention the quince and acacia, the pines and cedars.

It comes as no surprise, then, to find that the deep sense of unity with the flow of the seasons that is so characteristic of Japan is reflected in its own floral calendar, or *hanagoyomi.* An elaborate system linking the blossoming of flowers and trees to the planting and harvesting of crops, it is said to have been introduced into Japan from China in the seventeenth century. To judge from the calendars themselves, with their many allusions to folk practices based upon careful observation of changes in the seasons, we may suppose that there had already been something similar in Japan before that time. Like a kind of *Farmers' Almanac,* the hanagoyomi reminds us that the flowering of the cherry trees signals that spring vegetables should be planted, that with the arrival of the *u no hana* (Japanese sunflower) the rice is ready to be transplanted, and so forth—a continuing dialogue with nature all year round.

These days, with greenhouses, agricultural institutes, satellite weather forecasts, and soil-temperature monitoring, the floral calendar may look like a quaint relic. But the vital link between man and the rhythms of nature persists. Last week we arranged *shōbu* (Japanese iris) for Boy's Day—that makes six years in Japan now. . . . Rainy season soon—must put away my winter clothes, mildew, damp. . . . *Ajisai* (hydrangia)—that little temple in Kamakura, plan a trip. . . . July, August—where did I put the bamboo blind? . . . In no time at all one arranges one's own hanagoyomi.

I sometimes wonder about the future of doing ikebana in California, where it always seems like spring, or in Arizona, out among the cactuses. My master tells me I can do it anywhere, anytime. Perhaps so. But I can easier imagine myself sitting by a swimming pool on New Year's Day, looking up at the palm trees and great bushes of gaudy bird-of-paradise, and dreaming nostalgically of the modest little narcissus pushing up through the snows of Japan.

Joseph S. Lapenta

Shinkansen, 新幹線

The superexpress bullet train.

The bullet train it is called in English, and its statistics are well known: normal running speed of over two hundred kilometers an hour; one and a half billion passengers carried in fifteen years' operation without a single fatal accident; 240 trains per day, to be expanded greatly when new routes to the north of Tokyo are opened.

But after a while in Japan you take all that for granted. Going to Osaka? Just head for Tokyo Station, jump on a bullet (they leave at ten to fifteen minute intervals), and three hours and 515 kilometers later you are there. To get to Fukuoka, 1,069 kilometers away, takes four hours longer, but still not long enough to finish a good paperback. Usually you don't even have to worry about making a booking.

It's the smaller details you notice. What do twelve hundred or more people, cooped together on the world's fastest land transport, do with themselves? No, they don't look at the view. Most of it is factories, towns, and tunnels anyway, and while the route cuts right across the foot of Mount Fuji, the peak is usually covered with clouds. Some read, some eat, but most seem to share that curious Japanese ability to go immediately to sleep the moment they board anything moving, and to wake up just before their destination. Given the speed and occasional lurching, that is quite a feat.

Then there are the telephone announcements. Japanese businessmen who feel they can't afford to be out of circulation for even the short span it takes to get from one station to another, can for a small fee have their calls radioed into the train. There they are paged publicly and a whole train is left to wonder what urgent message awaits Mr. Suzuki of XYZ Company (you are identified either by your firm or your town).

But mainly it is the simple practicality of it all that strikes you. None of the romance and mystery of the Orient Express, though Tokyo-Fukuoka is farther than Paris-Zagreb. None of the fuss and

polish of the London-Edinburgh Flyer, which takes the best part of a day to get you a little farther than Tokyo-Osaka. Passengers sit in tight rows three and two abreast. Lunch boxes and canned drinks are trundled up and down the aisles by young, "take-it-or-leave-it" girls. A simple dining car features the ubiquitous curry-rice and hamburger steak.

At the end of the line, the remaining passengers are hustled off in a minute or so, a speedy clean-up crew gives the train a good once-over, and in no time at all it is heading back to the other end of Japan. All rather like a giant yo-yo bobbing up and down on a thin steel ribbon.

Of course, when you think about it, the reality is far from humdrum—several thousand tons of metal, luggage, and humanity being hurled across Japan at the speed of a small aircraft. The only hint you get is the sudden whoosh of air as you enter a tunnel, the cacophony of light as you pass another of these sleek monsters heading the other way, and the blur of . . . what was it, Hamamatsu? Shizuoka?

Gregory Clark

Tsuyu, 梅雨

The rainy season, also called *baiu*.

Forty days and forty nights of sopping saturation, dank, clammy, moldy, and gray—that is the way *they* often speak of it. However, this is going to be a minority report. I *like* the rainy season.

Actually, it is the gift of the gods: an extra season from mid-June to mid-July so placed as to temper the exuberance of spring and to slow the mad rush into the heat of summer. A reprieve from excess, a time for repose and contemplation of how nature achieves its harmony, which, of course, is always by compromise.

If it is really so nasty, why is it that the Japanese have given it such a lovely name—*tsuyu* or *baiu,* both of which can be written to mean the "plum rains."

Our plane left California in brilliant sunshine, and the last visual memory of the continent was a terrain of vivid reds, yellows, and browns. Most of the passengers were young Japanese in business suits, a sample of that postwar crowd returning from their first trips overseas. Later, when the pilot began the approach into Narita, there was a clamor at the windows. Out of the mist below us land appeared in the subdued hues of a lush vegetation. The crowd was silent until someone said in a hushed but distinct tone: *"Yappari aoi kuni da!"* ("It *is* a green country!")

Yes, it *is,* outstandingly so. This is probably due more than anything else to the annual rainfall of 1,800 millimeters, which is twice the world average. But not all of that comes pouring down. Indeed, the precipitation of the rainy season is typically—one might say fundamentally—of a very gentle sort, often to the point of being invisible. Call it, rather, moisture, or if you will, humidity. It serves the greenery perfectly in that it doesn't wash out to the sea as heavy rainfall does, Japan's rivers being notably short and swift. Here is nature compensating.

A world-traveling photographer once told me he found the quality of the Japanese atmosphere lost in his pictures unless he used Japanese lenses. I asked him to identify that quality. Gentle, he said, and then he began adding: mild, soft, balmy, calm, tranquil, amicable. These, as it happens, are all given in standard Japanese-English dictionaries in attempts to render the singular Japanese word *odayaka.* For there is nothing so pleasing to Japanese tastes as something that is odayaka—weather, for example, or a person. Naturally this applies to the tsuyu, as well as to those kindly souls influenced by its spell.

Yappari aoi kuni da. As is well known, *aoi* covers the vague range of blue-green, the most odayaka of colors in nature. Following the botanical calendar, it is just as things are beginning to get a bit garish that the tsuyu comes, bringing the blue-on-green iris and hydrangea and the "contrast" of the soft white gardenia.

I wonder what the Japanese temperament would be like if there were no tsuyu.

Holloway Brown

Rajio-taisō, ラジオ体操

Radio calisthenics.

Ichi–ni–san–shi!

If you happen to be walking near one of the thousands of neighborhood parks in Tokyo or any of Japan's other cities at 6:30 A.M. chances are you will hear the sound of voices counting out that familiar 1-2-3-4 rhythmic beat.

Drawing closer, you are likely to come upon a group of people, mostly elderly, doing exercises in unison. The piercing voice calling out the movements comes from a radio that someone has brought along. The sight is the same no matter what the season, how dark and cold the morning.

These early morning exercise sessions in parks and sandlots are part of an informal institution centered on a daily radio-exercise program almost as old as broadcasting itself. Inspired by an American radio program sponsored by a life-insurance company, Japan's public broadcasting system, NHK, began the ten-minute radio-exercise program, called *radio-taisō,* in 1928; and except for six years during the occupation, it has continued without interruption ever since.

This is all part of the special role that regular exercise has come to have in the lives of a large number of Japanese, and as such has been promoted by the Life Insurance Bureau of the Ministry of Posts and Telecommunications. Factories and other worksites commonly have a brief exercise period once or twice during the day; schoolchildren gather in the schoolyard to do exercises. That taisō is usually a group activity is probably a manifestation of the much-discussed Japanese penchant for doing things in groups, and perhaps, too, it's just more fun that way. In any case, these broadcast calisthenics provide an organized program of exercise for those who do not get it elsewhere.

The broadcast is repeated several times during the day, but the 6:30 A.M. program has long drawn the biggest audience. Many people do the exercises in the privacy of their homes, of course, but those who venture out regularly to join a taisō group make

new friends and feel an added sense of neighborliness. Some of the longstanding groups mark holidays and other festive occasions with refreshments, and these groups become the basis for other social or community activities. Schoolchildren are encouraged to participate during their summer holidays and receive prizes for perfect attendance.

The ten-minute exercise routine consists of a dozen varieties of rhythmical movements designed to be enjoyed by anyone, anywhere, any time.

The voice exhorting the faithful to stretch, bend, reach, twist, and turn is not the soft and coaxing voice one often hears on televised exercise programs. The announcer changes occasionally, but he always seems to have the same voice—that of a retired army drill sergeant. It is said that more than one rajio-taisō regular has been recruited accidentally when his radio dial fell upon the 6:30 A.M. exercise program: no one confronted with that voice could possibly stay in bed!

Susan Schmidt

Asagao, 朝顔

Morning glory.

On a late August morning some ten years ago in the old city of Kanazawa, I saw a trellis of *asagao* that I don't think I shall ever forget: purple, scarlet, azure, and white flowers, with petals as fragile as butterfly wings, brightly shining against a background of dark green leaves. To the Americans the "morning glory" and to the Japanese the "face of morning," this relative of the bindweed was brought to Japan from China in the Nara period. It seems that it was not until the Edo period, however, that the Japanese fell in love with its beauty and, of course, began to express it in their poetry. When the Edo-period poet Kaga no Chiyo awoke one morning to find that during the night the asagao had overgrown her well, she recorded her delight in these famous lines:

Asagao ni	The morning glory came
Tsurube torarete	And took away my well bucket.
Moraimizu.	I had to borrow water.

Between 1804 and 1839, if one is to believe the literature of the time, 180 kinds of flowers and over forty types of leaves were cultivated by enthusiastic gardeners of the asagao. Admirers of the frail but brightly colored blossom used to rise before dawn—and still do—to sit before their clay pots, or to rush to morning-glory markets, just to watch it burst into bloom.

The asagao one finds most often today is called *tairin,* or "large-wheeled" morning glory. A skilled grower can produce a blossom measuring from twenty to twenty-four centimeters in diameter. Names like purple *fuji,* crimson dragon, praise of heaven, and bamboo snow describe the variety of moods that can be created by this single flower. And as enthusiasts in the Edo period well knew, much time must be devoted to picking out just the right seeds to produce petals of unique shape.

At this point I have a confession to make. The flower branded on my memory from Kanazawa was not the Japanese but the American morning glory—for I saw it quite late in the morning. The Japanese asagao comes to full bloom at about 4 A.M. and by

9 has already faded, while the American variety lasts until noon. The Japanese, who seem especially fond of fleeting beauty and esteem it as the image of life itself, treasure this characteristic of their asagao. In the words of the famous haiku of Masaoka Shiki:

Asagao ya	The morning glory,
E ni kaku uchi ni	Even as I paint it,
Shiorekeri.	Fades away.

Ruth Linhart

Bon-odori, 盆踊

The summer Bon Festival folk dances.

When the spirits of the ancestors return to earth and prayers are offered for past, present, and future existences, it is only fitting that the visiting souls be welcomed and comforted—and what better way than with music and dancing.

Until the late fourteenth century it seems that members of the community, imitating the wanderings of the spirits, went from door to door offering prayers and ritualized dances for the benefit of household ancestors. Gradually, ceremonial robes became less solemn, and bright votive lanterns were gaily displayed to receive and dispatch the "special guests" of the evening. With time, the singing of ballads became an integral part of the activities and the atmosphere of the memorial service gave way to that of the festive celebration that Bon has now become.

Today, welcoming the family ancestors is largely a personal affair—to be observed or disregarded. But *bon-odori* seems to be enjoying a general, widespread revival. The reasons are not hard to understand. Dancing outdoors under the warm and starry summer sky is a treat in itself. Even if the music is electronically amplified, in the grounds of a temple, a schoolyard, or even a parking lot, there are no walls or roof to give it a "disco" atmosphere. The colored lanterns, the smells of soy sauce, roasted corn, and barbecued squid, and the throngs of men, women, and children attired in light *yukata* (cotton summer kimono) all combine to create a carnival mood.

Bon-odori itself is simple. A high scaffolding is erected in the middle of an open space. At least one large drum is mounted on a platform to accompany the music—taped or live. If the platform is large enough, a band of "model" dancers, usually members of a local dance club, will lead the crowd from that vantage point. Otherwise they will form a small ring about the base of the scaffolding and there perform the repetitive, easy-to-learn steps and hand motions making up the various dances. The rest of the participants form larger rings and simply follow the lead of the inner

circle. No one dances with a partner; the group dances as a unit. Because the steps tend to lead in a general counterclockwise direction, the effect is that of a giant brightly colored human wheel turning gently about the hub of the music platform.

And so it is that each August, as has been the custom for centuries, millions of Japanese—leaving behind their study, their work—make the pilgrimage home to join with the local community as it entertains its departed souls with music and dance.

Wayne Murphy

Taifū, 台風

Typhoon.

The typhoon is one of the things that come every year, a sign of the season. Though there are typhoons in the summer, it is an autumnal thing.

Among the more admirable qualities of the Japanese is an ability to pay fond attention to all the moods and signs of the seasons, including unpleasant and even baneful ones. In a fine modern novel, the chief beauty of which is its evocation of the Tokyo summer, even the mosquitoes are welcomed for their contribution

to the summeriness. In *The Tale of Genji* there is one major natural disaster, a typhoon; and the remarkable thing about it is that it does not seem all that disastrous. It serves to emphasize the evanescent beauty of an autumn garden.

Typhoons do not strike the most heavily populated parts of Japan every year, but they do strike somewhere, with such similar effects that the newspapers could, if they wished, use the same reports every year, changing only the proper nouns and the casualty figures. I used to think it odd that typhoons seemed to come as a fresh surprise every year, and that no one ever seemed prepared for them.

Then, flying in from Korea one afternoon, it struck me that in some respects the preparation is very thorough indeed. Korean rivers flow wild, taking whatever mountains and meadows they wish to. Japanese rivers are carefully tamed, kept within walls and deprived of their freedom. It is chiefly because of typhoons that the taming is necessary.

So careful in the matter of controlling rivers, the preparation seems wholly inadequate in the matter of building houses; and from the contrast may be built theories about Japanese culture.

It would be quite possible to build houses that would resist typhoons with fair success, but it would mean drawing a firm and clear line between indoors and outdoors. It would mean destroying what is most Japanese about a Japanese house.

Today, of course, dwellings are being built that do better resist typhoons; but the fact that for the most part they are by Western standards so badly built may arise from an assumption that they will presently be blown away or shaken or burned down in any event. If the penchant for ramshackle buildings has made Tokyo one of the world's more unsightly cities, the assumption has had admirable results too. The sense of evanescence continues to be very strong in this country, and it means that people do not take material objects too seriously. If something is going to blow away one day soon, why worry about it?

I am sure that when we run out of petroleum the shock will, for this reason, be less for the Japanese than for the other "developed nations."

Edward G. Seidensticker

Undōkai, 運動会

A game and exercise meet.

Once a year, in the autumn, Japan sets aside a day for the nationwide celebration of physical exercise through sports, games, and fun. Nearly every level of society–school, university, neighborhood, company, and village–arranges its own meets with a cooperative enthusiasm that seems geared to allow no one to escape participation. English has a hard time coming up with a good equivalent for *undōkai.* The literal rendering, "meeting for movement," is quaint but unacceptable; and the common dictionary definition of "athletic meet" does not suggest that while there are sporting events, and prizes awarded to the winners, the emphasis is not on winning according to the laws of athletic orthodoxy, but on exercise, cooperative spirit, and just plain having fun.

As things go in Japan, the undōkai has a relatively short history, tracing its origins to the educational reforms that marked the beginning of this century. Most events are still organized around schools, but the participants are not limited to the students. The undōkai is a community or neighborhood event. Local merchants contribute prizes. Citizenry in general as well as parents, teachers, and students all take part. Frequently it is the students themselves who are put in charge of planning and organizing the day. There will be races and other track-and-field events, but also events valued more for their humor–blindfold competitions, sack races, etc. Students take special delight in seeing their parents and teachers strain to compete under devilish conditions designed especially for them. Even a nursery school undōkai will feature games for teachers and parents, both on their own and together with the children.

A large university may hold its meet in a large stadium. I once witnessed a Waseda University undōkai held in the facilities built for the 1964 Olympic Games. In spite of the increase in scale, the emphasis on exercise, fun, and community spirit remained the same. In the Waseda meet, the athletic events were supplemented by such things as races featuring large students on small tricycles.

On whatever level the undōkai is organized, the events are not restricted to competitions, or even mock competitions, but frequently include such things as folk dancing as well. Cooperation and participation, then, are the essential ingredients of the undōkai. It is a celebration of community relatively free of the stratification that marks so much of Japanese social life, a kind of return to the basic sense of "moving together" that is the very soul of Japan.

Richard Wood

Miyamairi, 宮参り

The first visit of a newborn baby to its tutelary shrine.

Miyamairi is one of those things in Japan that make the foreign observer wonder whether the inhabitants of this island are the most religious or the least religious people in the world. From its literal meaning of a visit to a Shinto shrine, miyamairi has taken on the specific connotation of the presentation of a newborn infant to the local shrine of the *ubusuna no kami,* or deity of the locale in which one is born. It is the occasion on which the taboos associated with birth are lifted. Although customs differ considerably from place to place, a male child is generally taken to the shrine on the thirty-second day after birth, and a female child on the thirty-third. (Whether this implies that the family of a girl needs an extra day to be rid of the taboos that her birth inflicted on its environment must remain an open question.) Nowadays, however, most any sunny Sunday afternoon will do for both sexes—at least as long as it is not too inauspicious a day according to the ancient and complicated calendar to which the Japanese still fervently cling.

Many of the particular customs that traditionally accompanied the miyamairi and provided much local color are now well on their way to oblivion. For example, places where the shrine visit is still completed by making an equally reverential visit to the deity of the household toilet and pretending to feed the baby some excrement with chopsticks are largely unknown save to specialists in Japanese folklore. But that the essentials have been preserved is something any visitor can discover. For miyamairi carries far more symbolic persuasiveness than simply registering at the town hall. In the *norito,* or prayer recited by the Shinto priest, the child is formally welcomed into the community in which the gods and the people live harmoniously together. The mother or guardian carrying the baby might then respond by pinching the buttocks of the godchild in order to elicit an appropriate token of assent. Whether all of this deserves to be labeled "religious" seems to be a problem that is left for foreigners to worry about. In any event, it shows how the age-old traditions of Shinto, as a celebration of life full of the symbols necessary to express group unity, not only have not lost their significance but have weathered modernity remarkably well. As long as babies are brought to shrines, and as long as family and friends are given the chance to reaffirm this togetherness–aided, of course, by the spiritual invigoration of saké and other beverages essential to the celebration–life will always be stronger than death, and this country of Japan will survive together with its gods.

Jan Swyngedouw

Haiku, 俳句

A Japanese poem composed of three lines of five, seven, and five syllables respectively.

Haiku poetry is one of the art forms in which the Japanese sense of beauty is seen at its very best. It is also an art form whose development is Japanese and owes nothing much to either China or the West.

A haiku poem consists of seventeen syllables, usually divided into three lines of five, seven, and five syllables respectively. Some suggestion of the season is essential. Occasionally subtle, it is also often clear, as in the following lines by Yosa Buson (1716–83):

Haru no umi The sea in the spring—
Hinemosu notari All day long it rises and falls,
Notari kana. Just rises and falls.

Most important is the picture of the inner state of the poet caused by what he sees or hears or feels in the here and now. Delicate in sensitivity and deep in sentiment, the haiku is yet both restrained and subdued in its expression. It points to the heart of things, conveying experience without analyzing it. Haiku is a mirror image of reality, born out of the indescribable sense of being caught up in the wonder of life. The poet does not attempt to describe what he feels but to awaken this feeling in the reader by means of a few, masterly chosen words. The aesthetic asceticism of haiku abhors the dispensable word in the same way that *ikebana,* or flower arranging, abhors the inessential bud or leaf, or that Nō abhors the superfluous gesture, or that *sumi-e* (ink painting) abhors the unnecessary splash of ink. Consider this poem by the greatest of all haiku poets, Matsuo Bashō (1644–94):

Yoku mireba Carefully looking,
Nazuna hana saku Blooming shepherd's purse
Kakine kana. Under the hedge.

In the perfection of the art of haiku there is no separation of poet from poem. Sensations and perceptions reflect themselves through words in such a way that we might say the poet writes himself into the poem through his experience, manifesting the unity between himself and the world he reflects. For these reasons, the reader of haiku is not only expected to admire the poem as a creation of its author's genius; he must also actively recreate in himself the author's original experience. To read haiku, then, one must become a poet oneself.

Yūzuki ya The evening moon—
Ume chirikakaru Plum blossoms falling
Koto no ue. On a lute.

Written nearly eight decades ago by the poet Masaoka Shiki, such verses survive the ravages of time with no loss of freshness or vitality. Just as the Japanese plum tree has taken root in many a Western country, so too will the Japanese haiku bloom wherever there are people true to the poet in their hearts.

Vladimir Devidé

Yukimizake, 雪見酒

Drinking saké while enjoying the snow.

In the spring, cherry blossoms,
in the summer the cuckoo,
in autumn the moon,
And in winter the snow, clear, cold.
—Dōgen

The pleasures of cherry-blossom viewing are well known, and many have heard the solitary call of a cuckoo in summer or gazed on the bright moon of autumn. Fewer, however, have experienced the beauty of snow viewing, which somehow seems less inviting than the others. Yet snow viewing is perhaps the most singularly Japanese of all. Cherry-blossom festivals are celebrated overseas, beautiful birds live in all countries, and the full moon shines everywhere; but what other place has such fine white snow? The severe cold and the heavy moist air make Japanese snow rich and frothy, almost like the thick ceremonial tea.

Although saké knows no seasonal limits, it has a special affinity with snow viewing. Saké is best when heated, and on a cold winter's night it warms the hands, the mouth, and the heart. In northern Japan, some villages are snowed in for the entire winter, and the inhabitants spend much of their seclusion sitting around the hearth contemplating the snow. Still better is snow viewing from an outdoor hot-spring pool.

Japanese temples are most beautiful in winter and are favorite places for snow viewing. It has been my custom to spend New Year's Eve working at a mountain temple where, from midnight until late the next evening, worshipers come to ring the temple bell, to offer prayers for the New Year, and to buy fortunes and *omamori* talismans. I recall one particular year when a silver-white snow had fallen throughout the night. The snow reflected the glow of the temple lights and the shadows of the worshipers as they gently moved to each little shrine surrounding the main hall. In the icy air the muffled tones of bells and wooden drums mixed with festive voices full of New Year's greetings could be heard.

Around four in the morning the number of worshipers decreased and the priests had an hour or so before the crowds returned at daybreak. In that coldest hour of the night they gathered around the old hibachi, warming their hands, eating rice cakes, sipping the first saké of the year, and looked out at the softly falling snow. Gradually the frigid darkness lifted as the snow, pure and serene, blanketed the entire mountain. Indeed it seemed as if the sky, the mountain, and the snow all blended together to form a vibrant landscape that somehow embraced the lives of the priests and worshipers there. Such is the miracle of *yukimizake*.

John Stevens

Shiwasu, 師走

The end-of-the-year rush, also the old name for December.

The first time I heard the word *shiwasu* was during my first year of teaching at a Japanese university. Preparing class lectures took longer in those days, since I was new at the business and had to give much more time to correcting student reports and essays. Meanwhile, I was trying to finish my dissertation for an American university. And on top of everything, I was living in a student

dormitory on campus, where visitors popped in at any hour of the day or night.

In December of that year I recall how the occasional visitor who dropped in would glance across the top of my desk, note the typewriter paused in mid-sentence, scan the piles of books, papers, reports, unaddressed greeting cards, and then utter something apologetic about "shiwasu" before settling down for an hour's discussion or more. After the word had reappeared three or four times, I finally got around to asking somebody what it meant. My informant said that shiwasu was an old name for the last month of the year—the busiest one for teachers (*shi*) who have to do so much rushing around (*hasu* or, euphonically, *wasu*). Then he poured himself another cup of coffee and settled back for a chat.

Fortunately there were only two hundred and fifty students in the dormitory, some of them as busy as I, so that it was possible to get some work done. A few deadlines were not met, some reports were late in being returned, and greeting cards were mailed after New Year's—but somehow, in a human sort of way, things got done.

Scholars of the Japanese language are not sure of the exact origin of the expression "shiwasu," but it appears at least as far back as the Heian period in the *Pillow Book* of Sei Shōnagon. It is conjectured that the word referred to the hectic time the Buddhist monks had during the last month of the year, constantly called on to perform rites and services.

When I consider how my own Decembers are spent, and when I look around at my busy colleagues, it strikes me that although the amount of time available has not increased much, the meaning of shiwasu has changed somewhat. Besides all the usual labors associated with university teaching, December brings *bōnenkai:* a seemingly endless round of parties to end the year. Of course, it may well be that ritual get-togethers with colleagues, students, and former students are an important part of the educational process, just like those conversations over coffee in the dormitory. And if one considers personal contact between teacher and student as an essential ingredient in education, the December "busyness" of teachers in Japan could possibly be their finest hour.

William Currie

Shio, 塩

Salt.

Few things in human culture can claim the age, the universality, and the enduring value that belong to salt. Its uses as a condiment and a preservative have made it an important commodity from ancient times. The sites of its production were among the first centers of trade, from which commercial networks of "salt routes" spread out far and wide. Towns like Saltwich in England and Shiojiri in Japan owe their names to such salt commerce. Perhaps because of its importance to human life, salt also came to acquire a sacred, ritual significance as well, through which it finds its way into innumerable maxims, tales, traditions, and religious ceremonials throughout the world.

In Japan salt has long been viewed as a means of purification and a source of magical power. The former association may ultimately be related to the fact that Japanese salt is extracted from the sea, where ancient ceremonial cleansings were performed. The inhabitants of Okinawa, on returning from a funeral, still bathe in the sea to rid themselves of the impurity of death. It is the general custom all over Japan to have a family member scatter salt at the entrance of the house before the mourners enter, to protect them from contamination through contact with the dead. It has even become a custom in recent years for the family of the deceased to distribute small packets of salt to the mourners themselves for this purpose.

Inextricably linked with the purifying function of salt is its magical use, which can be seen in such customs as *mori-jio,* the placing of a small mound of salt at a restaurant entrance to ensure that no evil enters. Mori-jio can also be observed in agricultural households at the time of the New Year festivities, when the salt is set alongside the well or hearth. After an unwelcome guest has departed, someone may say, "Throw out some salt!" Whether or not it is actually done, the meaning is one of good riddance. In the same sense salt is commonly scattered before religious processions and is used in some exorcism services. Perhaps the best example of the way the purifying and magical powers of salt combine is to be seen in the ritual of salt-scattering accompanying sumo wrestling. Although tradition ascribes this to an ancient Shinto purification ritual, I sometimes wonder if it doesn't enter the minds of the wrestlers to think of it as a way to gain control over the enemy.

Gaynor Jenke

Umeboshi, 梅干

Pickled plums.

From the moment that the *ume,* or Japanese plum, comes into flower, I begin looking forward to those days in early June when greengrocers will display its hard, green, unripe fruit. Tougher than octopus, intolerably sour, and no doubt as unwholesome as unripe apples, the green ume are inedible–and yet vast quantities of this seemingly useless fruit are marketed each year. But they are never sold ripe.

A good deal of ume go into making *umeshu,* or plum liqueur. When matured, in a year or two, both the umeshu and the ume are of considerable medicinal value–for example, as a preventive or specific for constipation. But by far the greatest part of ume are turned into *umeboshi,* the soft pickled plums that are the perfect complement to a fresh bowl of rice.

Like so many other things in Japan, the preparation of umeboshi marks the passing of a season. The green ume are washed, soaked, transferred to a stoneware vat, sprinkled liberally with salt, and weighted down to marinate in their own juices for about two weeks. Just before the rainy season sets in, the freshly picked leaves of the red, mintlike *shiso* are rubbed in salt and added to the vat to contribute their subtle flavor and to color the ume. During the rainy season the leaves and ume marinate quietly. By the time it is over the ume are soft and red right through to their stones and can be removed from the vat and let to stand outside to dry for two or three days in the fresh, clear air. After drying, the umeboshi are stored in a clean vat, ready for eating or for aging to be eaten later. Since umeboshi are never attacked by bacteria or mold, a season's yield can be enjoyed for many years.

Umeboshi are such an important dietary staple in Japan that it is said one can survive as long as one has an umeboshi and a bowl of rice. Indeed, during the war years many people did subsist on just that. Even today one of the most familiar packed lunches is a single umeboshi in a bed of rice—called the *hinomaru bentō* ("rising-sun lunch") because of its resemblance to the national flag.

But more than tradition recommends umeboshi to the diet. Although green ume are acidic, the salted umeboshi are alkaline and hence offer an ideal neutralizer for the acidity of animal proteins. Moreover, they effectively prevent the stomach upset that can result from eating food that is not quite as fresh as it looks, which is comforting knowledge in a hot, humid country where unrefrigerated food can quickly go bad.

Ranging in taste from extremely salty-sour to tart with the faintest hint of sweetness, the umeboshi can satisfy a wide variety of preferences and are open to adaptations in flavor by making adjustments in the recipe. It took me a few years to find the piquant umeboshi that I like best, but I now find them so indispensable that a diet without them seems somehow unhealthy, uninteresting, and bland. Possibly I, too, could survive as long as I have an umeboshi and a bowl of rice.

Rebecca M. Davis

Kaisō, 海藻

Algae; seaweed.

The image of the lovely young country girl wading through the shallows in her scarlet kimono to gather the rich harvest of *kaisō* from the ocean's garden is one of the most enchanting pictures of daily life drawn in the eighth-century poetic anthology *Man'yō-shū.* Since ancient times the Japanese have enjoyed more vegetables from the sea than any other people in the world. From the graceful twisted strands of *wakame* invariably floating in the morning's *miso* soup to the pressed dried sheets of *nori* wrapping

sushi rolls to the sea gelatin *tengusa* (agar) to the little "deer tails" of seasoned *hijiki* to well over a dozen varieties of the big flat kelps, or *konbu,* the Japanese recommend sea vegetables for taste, health, beauty, and dietary and aesthetic reasons. Legend has it that the elixir of immortality so eagerly sought by Chinese emperors was to be found in konbu, and modern research has established a correspondence between a diet based primarily on sea foods and long life in Japan.

The sea vegetables belong to the simplest plant classification, algae, of which there are some 8,000 known species in the world. Among these the Japanese consume approximately 220 species from the green group, 270 from the brown, and 670 from the red. Most of these were known and treasured by the Japanese as early as the seventh century.

So closely are we linked with our mother the sea that the very constitution of our blood is reflected in the mineral-salt balance of the ocean. Algae have the amazing property of absorbing concentrates of these minerals directly and creating vitamins and proteins capable of sustaining people in times of starvation. Their seemingly magical efficacy against certain diseases—hijiki was found to give thick, glossy hair and a clear complexion, and konbu helps prevent hardening of the arteries—has long been known by the Japanese. And since it contains practically no calories yet is sufficiently filling, seaweed has been hailed as the answer to the dieter's prayers. With the new health-food and dieting consciousness of recent years, Americans have been rushing to join the ranks of kaisō beneficiaries, and in the process have found renewed interest in Japanese cooking.

The Japanese, meanwhile, continue as they have done for centuries to offer thanks on major occasions for *yama no sachi, umi no sachi,* the blessings of the land and the blessings of the sea. Anyone fortunate enough to have spent New Year's in Japan will recall the round, cushionlike dumplings (*kagami mochi*) that represent the yama no sachi. And whatever variations there be from region to region, the one symbol of the munificence of the sea accompanying mochi throughout the islands of Japan is, of course, kaisō.

Sharon Ann Rhoads

Daizu, 大豆

Soybeans.

The story is told of Ogyū Sorai (1666–1728), one of the outstanding scholars of the Edo period and official tutor to the shogun, that when he was young and poor, he could afford nothing to eat but *okara,* the lees of *tōfu* (soybean curd). The tōfu maker would occasionally take pity on him and treat Sorai to a feast of fresh tōfu. But far from being inhibited by this okara diet, the young man thrived on the protein-rich food and went on to become a giant among scholars. Or so the story goes.

The great soybean triumvirate–soy sauce, *miso* (fermented bean paste), and tōfu–towers high in Japanese cooking. Soy sauce and miso provide the salt and flavor for soups and sauces as well as for stewed, baked, grilled, and sautéed foods. The custardlike consistency of tōfu and its blandness (it was formerly written with ideograms that meant "white wall") lend themselves well to the variety of methods known for preparing and seasoning it. Tōfu can be eaten cooked or uncooked, mashed or whole, pressed or dried. Given its bulk and high protein content, it can even become the main ingredient of a meal, as it did for Sorai.

While many tōfu recipes originated in the temples of Japan where monks were forbidden to eat meat, tōfu itself dates back some two thousand years in China. One recipe, that for dried *kōya-dōfu,* is said to have been invented by Japanese monks of the twelfth century and later adopted in China in the eighteenth century.

In addition to soy milk and soy oil, another soybean derivative is *yuba,* the skin that forms on the surface when soy milk is cooked slowly. This byproduct, which contains even more protein than tōfu, takes on a chewy quality when dried and re-cooked.

The body of knowledge, cooking techniques, and lore that has grown up around the soybean throughout East Asia would fill volumes. Japanese mythology has it that when Ōgetsu-hime, the goddess of grains, was slain, rice, wheat, red beans, millet, and soybeans issued forth from her body orifices. (The soybean came

into the world from her derrière.) Less ignominious and more historical accounts inform us that it originated in China and passed through Korea before reaching Japan.

Although soy sauce and miso will keep for some time without refrigeration, tōfu is highly perishable, and even today is eaten soon after purchase. Okara and soy milk are not as common as they were before World War II, but it is still possible to find housewives who use them regularly in cooking. In fact, a woman may even still polish her floors and pillars with okara, which gives them a special smooth sheen.

Despite its ancient pedigree, this little bean that Ōgetsu-hime gave to the world is not eulogized in Japanese literature. But, as an old song from the Edo period reminds us, it holds a vital place in the life of the people:

The nightingale stays far from the crowds;
Twelve kilometers from the saké shop,
Eight kilometers from the tōfu shop.

Patricia Murray

Yakumi, 薬味

Condiments.

Plump, white Chinese *udon* noodles glisten in scalding fragrant broth. Slices of braised chicken nestling with brilliant green swatches of blanched spinach and pieces of lotus root, fish cake, mushroom, and young kelp combine to arouse the most listless appetite. But even this mouth-watering dish is surprisingly bland and uninteresting without the all-important addition of *yakumi.* A sprinkling of toasted sesame seeds, a liberal helping of finely chopped chivelike greens, a dash of ground red pepper, a dab of grated ginger root–these unobtrusive condiments are as essential to Japanese noodle dishes as salad dressing is to salad.

Yakumi are fresh or dried seasonings used to stimulate the appetite and enhance the flavor of foods. In traditional cooking, yakumi is a select and unchanging category of herbs that continue to form the pivot of Japanese cuisine, despite the variety of Western herbs and spices from South and Southeast Asia that have made their way into the diet.

Take *wasabi* (horseradish) for example–that diminutive light green pile on a plate of *sashimi* (raw-fish slices) or the pale stripe on sushi. This unassuming condiment, capable of clearing your sinuses and bringing you to tears in seconds if applied in excess, is essential to the enjoyment of raw fish and was even used in the days before refrigerators to combat bacteria and parasites.

Yakumi also add the final touch of excellence to steaming bouillabaisse-like *nabemono* dishes, a favorite during the winter months. A pot of carefully constructed stock or broth is set to boiling on the dinner table and filled with vegetables and meat or fish. When ready these are pulled from the pot and dipped in *tare,* a sauce made with soy sauce, saké, and whatever creative combination of sesame seed, grated ginger root, *daikon* (Japanese radish), diced onion greens, and the like is the specialty of the cook.

In the aristocratic canons of refined Japanese cuisine, yakumi are washed and grated, rinsed, and coddled into the attractive corners of the gourmet landscape. But they are also the friend of the busy student or truck driver on the move. A combination of skillfully blended condiments scattered liberally over a steaming bowl of rice and covered with hot green tea makes *o-chazuke,* a perfect late-night snack or even a substantial meal for the thin of pocket. If you think it sounds unsatisfying, you have not bargained on the illustrious qualities of yakumi, whose simple secrets create much of the joy of Japanese food.

Lynne E. Riggs

Donburi, 丼

A rice meal, served in a bowl.

The age-old riddle of whether the chicken is merely the egg's way of reproducing itself, or vice versa, comes to rest in Japan, appropriately, atop a steaming heap of rice in a scramble of chicken and eggs that the Japanese call *oya-ko donburi.* Whichever be *oya* (parent) and whichever *ko* (child), this meal in a bowl has come to be recognized as the classical form of Japanese fast food: the donburi.

The familiar trademark of the large chain of Yoshinoya donburi diners—"quick, tasty, cheap"—says it all. Gone are the elaborately landscaped ensembles of fish and pickles and vegetables for which the Japanese cuisine is famous. Gone, the whole array of dishes and plates and trays. And in their place, a plain, no-nonsense, thrifty lunch.

There are several varieties of donburi dishes, each taking its common name from the ingredients laid on top of the universal foundation of rice. For example, *katsu-don* uses slices of pork cutlets and eggs; *ten-don,* tempura; *gyū-don,* beef; *una-don,* eel; and so forth. Though there must be some inbuilt restrictions to the use of names and regional variations, to the outsider they are difficult to discern. I remember once ordering an oya-ko donburi and finding pork where there should have been chicken. On inquiring I was informed (or perhaps gotten the better of by a quick-witted proprietor) that I had received the next best thing: *mama-ko don* (stepparent and child donburi).

Donburi came into being around the time that Japan was starting off on its rush to industrialization, and yet fits equally well the city rat race or the leisurely country restaurant. An added attraction is that it is an easy meal to have delivered to one's home or place of business—just a phone call away. (In some cases, *too* easy. The young wife who too often has donburi sent around, instead of taking time to prepare a traditional meal, may find herself under the cloud of her mother-in-law's criticism.)

In spite of the growing tendency toward specialization in the restaurants of Japan, there are a few dishes that still seem to be available just about anywhere, and donburi is one of them. But to me, donburi always seems to taste best at the small, family-operated diner near my apartment. Everyone knows everyone else and the camaraderie adds to the flavor of the food.

A few years ago, the Yoshinoya chain went to the United States and began to open diners around the country. Like their Japanese motto, their American slogan seems to offer just the right introduction to this tasty little bowl from the Orient: "No waiting. No menu. No decisions. No check. No tipping. No kidding. Just lunch."

Edward J. Licht

Makudonarudo, マクドナルド

McDonald's restaurant-chain.

The Japanese taste for foreign food and drink is as much a part of its culture now as its own cuisine, and sometimes is even confused with it. The popular tempura, which was adapted from European fried food of the seventeenth century, is a case in point. The same could be said of sukiyaki, invented during the Meiji era in imitation of Western beef dishes. Even certain sweets that have come to be regarded as traditionally Japanese have European or Chinese origins. Whether the Japanese have grown more international in their tastes or whether it is simply that outside influence has reached the saturation point in the cuisine, there seem to be signs that this pattern of absorption by adaptation is breaking down in favor of simple absorption. Of this there is no better symbol in all of Japan than *Makudonarudo.*

The American visitor who passes under the familiar golden arches for the first time in Japan is surprised to find everything quite as he had left it at home. What is even more surprising is that the Japanese tourist to America can have the same experience. As one Japanese Boy Scout excitedly reported to his friends on returning from the World Jamboree in California: *"Amerika ni mo Makudonarudo ga aru!"* ("Even in America they have McDonald's!") Had he stopped in the branch in Santa Clara that is under direct management of McDonald's of Japan, his conviction that the Big Mac is a Japanese invention would probably have been deepened beyond redemption.

The $3 million worth of business done annually by the Ginza Mitsukoshi branch in Tokyo gives some idea of the success of Makudonarudo in Japan, though the average restaurant handles only about half that amount. Aside from the occasional addition (such as iced coffee and orange milkshakes) and omission (the breakfast menu, for instance), the menu is built around the same three pillars of hamburgers, fries, and shakes, and looks and tastes the same on both sides of the Pacific. The most conspicuous difference is that many Japanese Makudonarudo have little or no seating and average only about 270–300 square meters in size. But to a people accustomed to tight quarters and *tachigui* ("stand-up eating"), this is not the distraction it might be elsewhere. The rapid expansion from a single outlet in 1971 to 162 in 1978 should be proof enough.

Japanese tend to think of themselves as borrowers of culture. In fact the history of their interaction with China and the West has been less one of borrowing than of creative adaptation from which has come their own distinctive culture. In becoming Japanese, the food served by Makudonarudo has been borrowed, but the nature of the restaurants has been adapted to fit the realities of Japanese cities. At least in major cities, genuine Indian, Southeast Asian, and Western foods coexist with Japanese foods, just as Paris, London, and New York fashions can be found alongside the products of Japanese designers.

Richard Wood

Okosama-ranchi, お子様ランチ

A special children's lunch.

Which do your children prefer: airplanes, trains, or yachts? You may not be able to take them on a real trip each time they ask, but if you are in Japan you can do the next best thing: take them out to lunch. There, within the reach of any parent's pocketbook, they can be set free to fantasize a trip to exotic places while eating a feast especially concocted for the small fry: the *okosama-ranchi,* or children's lunch.

This special creation for children is served in any restaurant that caters to families, particularly those in department stores and other large establishments, and is designed to appeal to little appetites and big imaginations. On a plate shaped like anything from a spaceship to a teddy bear is an assortment of foods that are perennial kids' favorites—spaghetti, hamburger, pilaf, pancakes—and often a small toy that the child can take home. Topped with a flag (the Stars and Stripes, Japan's *Hinomaru,* or the Union Jack, and occasionally even the tricolors of France or Italy), the okosama-ranchi is a cut-rate splendor, an assortment that on the adult menu would empty your pocket.

Every department-store restaurant has excellent meals to attract the shopper, and meals for the shoppers' children are a logical extension of that appeal. A special lunch with a nutritionally balanced selection of foods, in small portions, attractively (even irresistibly) presented, may be the ideal answer to that universal parental headache: getting the kids to eat.

But there is evidence that little children are not the only ones benefiting from this ingenuity. Among the lunchtime crowds in Tokyo department-store restaurants, a number of young women are to be seen ordering okosama-ranchi. They explain that it's the best way to get a nourishing lunch that is modest in quantity and low in price at the same time.

The presence of the okosama-ranchi on restaurant menus dates back well before Japan's present-day prosperity. Many parents and grandparents remember the more austere version of their own

childhood: a scoop of rice with a few garnishes, but always that flag.

Nowadays it takes a lot to impress children who are wooed by toy and food manufacturers and catered to by doting relatives. But the restaurants are keeping up with the pace in Japan, devising ever more elaborate combinations for the okosama-ranchi.

Susan Schmidt

Ekiben, 駅弁

Box lunches sold on trains and at railway stations.

Anyone who has ridden on a train in Japan is familiar with the sight of vendors pushing carts of edibles up the aisle. A glance inside reveals a fairly standardized assortment: beer and soft drinks, fruit, nuts, crackers and dried squid (to go with the beer), a few magazines, and, finally, a stack of rather mysterious-looking boxes. These often elaborately wrapped parcels contain what the Japanese call *ekiben*—literally, "station lunches." Japan's extensive and flourishing railway system has helped the ekiben to reach a level of consumption of about two million per week.

The first ekiben was a simple but overpriced affair consisting of two plain rice balls and a few pickles wrapped in bamboo leaves and was sold on the Ueno-Utsunomiya line in 1885. At present there are said to be sixteen hundred varieties of ekiben served in as many different kinds of containers, ranging in price from the very cheap to the moderately expensive. The most popular, the *makunouchi,* is a smorgasbord in miniature, with around a dozen morsels—fish, meat, pickles, egg, and vegetables—apportioned in compartments and flanked by a white field of rice with a red sour plum in the middle—this last rather like the Japanese flag. The makunouchi is unusual in that it is sold all over the country, whereas other ekiben are generally identified according to their locality: Sendai's chestnut-rice meal, Gifu's sweetfish sushi, Kobe's meat-and-rice casserole, Yokokawa's "Mountain-Pass Rice Pot" (which comes in an earthenware pot), and on and on until practically every major railroad stop seems to have its own characteristic ekiben.

There are three elements involved in ekiben appreciation: how it looks, what it tastes like, and where it comes from. Visual aesthetics, stressed in so many areas of Japanese cuisine, are especially developed in the ekiben, where limitations of space and cost require great ingenuity in the designing of containers and the arranging of food. As for flavor, the fact that the ekiben are served cold presents no particular problem, since food is often eaten cold in Japan; it is the freshness and quality of the ingredients that are of importance. These in turn are related to the locale, for the ekiben is expected to be made up of produce from the local region. One suspects, however, that other things must be involved in the insistence on the use of regional products, for in this modern age of dry ice and rapid transport a few dozen kilometers is really of little consequence. Perhaps the reason is that for the Japanese traveler an ekiben is not just a meal but a way to establish a direct physical relationship with the area he happens to be passing through. The fish may have been caught in that bay over there, the greens picked on that mountain, the rice grown in that paddy. In this sense, then, the traveler is not restricted to merely watching the scenery pass by—he can eat it too.

Theodore Goossen

Manaita, まな板

The cutting board.

Tat-tat-tat-tat-tat. The sound of a knife on a cutting board. One imagines a woman intently slicing some cucumbers, which spill out from the edge of the knife. Or it could be a clean-shaven cook who with swift strokes is creating another culinary delight for the waiting customer.

Everything from the simplest dish to the most refined begins its career on the *manaita,* or cutting board. And it is there, too, that anyone who wishes to master the art of preparing Japanese food must begin an apprenticeship. The very word for cook–*itamae-san,* or person before the board–bears this out. There are dozens of ways to cut vegetables: razor-thin slices, cubes, strips as fine as

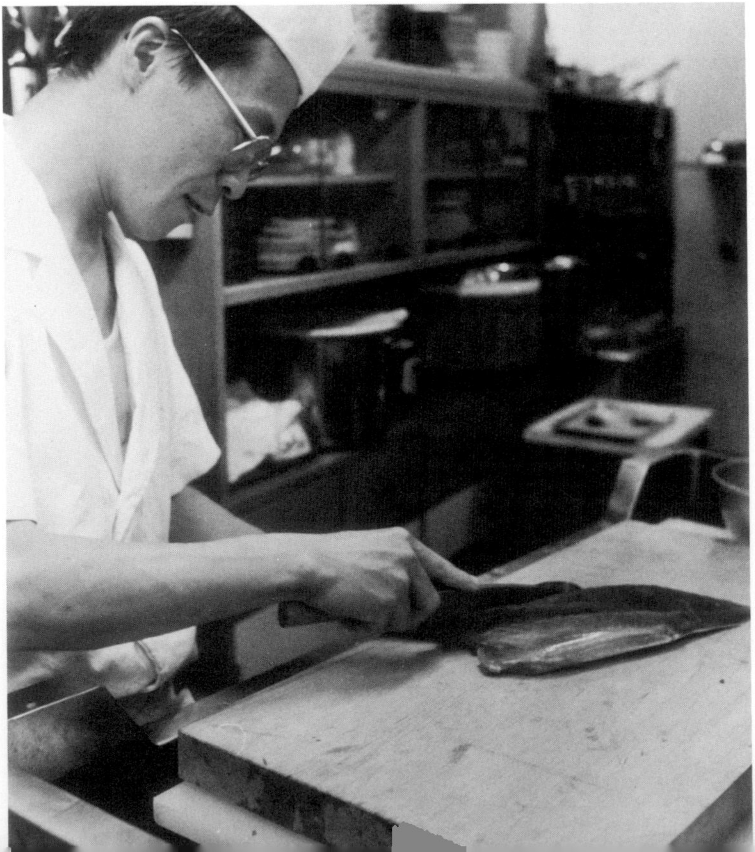

vermicelli, diamonds, "bamboo leaves," "pine needles," "plum blossoms," and on and on.

In Japanese cuisine, to speak of the "flavor of the shape," or *katachi no aji,* is an accepted form of praise. For it is not only the tongue that can taste, but the eyes as well. Texture, form, color, and arrangement all provide a flavor uniquely their own, which is why at formal meals one is expected to feast the eyes before feeding the stomach.

It is said that the art of cutting food with such admirable precision originated with the preparation of fish. In fact, manaita actually refers to a "fish board." Because fish demands expertise and the finest of knives (raggedly cut raw fish is found disgusting), the Japanese have developed a high degree of skill in the handling of knives—a skill that extends to the preparation of other foods as well. Another reason often mentioned is the use of chopsticks, which require that the food be served in bite-size pieces.

I would suggest, however, something more basic: Japanese resourcefulness. A cucumber cut in large chunks can hardly be satisfying. But once sliced into a multitude of transparent pale-green discs, it becomes an appetizing salad. In former days when food was far from abundant, the simple tools of knife and board could transform a scanty meal into a banquet.

Self-reliance, determination, perseverance, and imagination: these are what the manaita is made of. Could it not be, perhaps, that many of the technological marvels of contemporary Japan trace the roots of this discipline and its attention to detail to generations of children who grew up watching mothers preparing supper on the carving board?

My friends tell me that one's character is revealed in the way one works at the manaita. For example, sliced cucumbers that remain joined at one edge where the knife failed to reach are a sign of negligence and laziness. But, despite all my efforts, the moment I speed up to a brisk tat-tat-tat, the cucumber slices get stuck together. The day I manage to cut them flawlessly I shall consider myself among the masters of manaita and thoroughly Japanized as well. Meantime, I can display my badge of merit: the band-aid on my left thumb.

Patricia H. Massy

Shokuhin Sanpuru, 食品サンプル

Model food, displayed in glass cases at restaurants.

A Japanese city at meal time—such a variety of places to eat: main streets, back streets, shopping arcades, the top floors of department stores—all packed with restaurants large and small. As people stroll by, you see them pausing to peer in the front windows of these eating places before choosing one to enter. What are they examining so intently? Take a closer look. Each window is filled with a display of the food offered inside, a visual menu with the name and price beside each dish. The food looks quite real, but the discerning eye will soon detect an artificial luster, an overbrightness of color. They're all plastic! Welcome to the brave new world of Japanese handicraft at its best, and *shokuhin sanpuru.*

The idea of food samples originated in the late nineteenth century when some restaurants, caught up in the craze for things foreign, found it useful to advertise new and unfamiliar dishes by placing a sample out front for passers-by to see. Flies, animals, and a tendency to deteriorate were distinct disadvantages, but it was not until 1951 that the practice of sculpting samples came into being. The first models were made of painted wax but deteriorated rather rapidly, particularly during hot weather. In recent years improved techniques and the use of vinyl plastics have made food samples remarkably durable and lifelike—at times even more appetizing than the real thing itself.

Though the food-sample industry is a postwar phenomenon, its organization is not unlike that of the traditional crafts. Be it a large factory with a hundred employees or a small, family-based operation, the relationship between respected master and loyal associates is predominant. And the same powerful mystique of handicraft in Japan—that belief in the transcendental nature of any skill perfected through years of constant repetition—pervades the food-sample world as well. Three years of apprenticeship are required before the simpler models can be attempted, and another six to learn to make imitation sushi. Only the master will attempt the most difficult models, and everywhere trade secrets are jealously guarded.

The benefits for both restaurant and client are obvious, as are the perils of occasional discrepancies. But the only way to become a connoisseur is at the "gut level," where you let your stomach do the talking. Look at the noodles—no response. Look at the curry—nothing yet. Look at the broiled fish—faint stirrings. Look at the sushi . . . . And when you feel that deep inner rumbling, you know that this must be the place.

Theodore Goossen

Oshibori, おしぼり

A dampened towel served for the refreshment of guests or customers.

Unlike most parts of Europe and North America, Japan is an extremely humid country. The sultry summer heat can be a special trial. What could be more delightful, when visiting a friend on such a day, than to be offered a cool *oshibori,* that tightly wrung, slightly dampened, white oblong of cloth used to wipe one's face and hands? This, surely, is the epitome of hospitality. (In winter, of course, the oshibori is served steaming hot.) This thoughtful custom, which began as a courtesy to callers at private homes, was widely adopted by the restaurant trade after World War II—a compact washcloth, napkin, and finger bowl all in one.

The oshibori wipes away more than grime. It warms or cools,

soothes and refreshes, at least temporarily expunging care and stress. In its combination of practical function and psychological effect, the oshibori can be seen, indeed, as an outgrowth of the same mentality that created such Japanese arts as the tea ceremony.

Ever since the opening of Japan to the West in the latter half of the nineteenth century, the Japanese have eagerly imported a large variety of both goods and ideas from the West. In return, Japan has exported a great many goods—but so far, not many cultural artifacts. The oshibori is a rare exception and, in some modest way, helps rectify the lopsided imbalance of cultural trade.

Not surprisingly, Japan Air Lines was the first company to begin serving oshibori to passengers on international flights, thus introducing the custom to the outside world. So well received was this service that before long non-Japanese carriers began to follow suit. Now, on many flights in the United States, cabin attendants can be seen serving passengers with damp cloths, lifted antiseptically from a tray by means of tongs, as a kind of pre-meal courtesy.

Ironically, in Japan itself the oshibori is no longer the indispensable part of dining that it once was. It used to be that one was invariably served an oshibori along with a glass of water on entering even the humblest restaurant or coffee shop. Now, all too often, one gets nothing—or, at best, a simple rack of minuscule paper napkins good for nothing much but wiping up spilled coffee.

Of course, the oshibori is far from extinct in the land of its birth. It is still *de rigueur* at any Japanese-style restaurant worth its salt. Really well managed establishments, as well as cabarets and nightclubs with any pretensions of class, have a fresh oshibori awaiting the customers after every trip to the bathroom.

Providing oshibori for eating and drinking establishments is an industry in itself. Interestingly, commercial oshibori supply-and-cleaning service was introduced after the war, so I have been told, by a pair of enterprising Americans, whose names adorn the panel trucks that can still be seen going along the Tokyo streets: "Davenroy." If the story is true, Dave and Roy must be rich men by now.

Suzanne Trumbull

Yatai, 屋台

Movable nighttime street stalls selling food and drink.

At shrine or temple festivals, or in public parks, in the side streets near railway stations and amusement centers, or in the alleys of densely populated quarters—that is where you will find the *yatai.* These are the compact, wooden restaurants-on-wheels that first became popular in Japan a century ago, and from which are dispensed steaming-hot Japanese delicacies served with saké or beer.

A yatai is nothing more than a two-wheeled handcart to which have been added the basic facilities required for serving food and drink. Adjustable legs hold it level when not in motion. Handles for pulling it from place to place slide ingeniously into the body framework when not in use. The rear end has storage compartments rising up to support a solid roof. In these are kept dishes, bottles, food ingredients, sauces, condiments, fuels, and other supplies. Chopsticks, skewers, knives, and cooking utensils are available in a drawer at the front end between the handle shafts. The table for customers is a waist-high wooden surface into which there has been recessed either a hot plate or a copper-lined receptacle for soup heated from beneath.

The fare offered by the yatai ranges from Japanese or Chinese noodles and barbecued chicken to *oden.* This latter is a tasty assortment of different fish pastes in varied shapes, vegetables, boiled eggs, fried bean-curd cakes, seaweed, thick cross sections of boiled radishes, and other favorite Japanese foods—the whole kept simmering, immersed in a pungent broth, to be selected and eaten with or without mustard, to taste.

Inevitably, the yatai have been victimized by modern innovations and changing food fashions. The daytime customers are dwindling, satisfied perhaps with the impersonal services of vending machines, or lured away by the motorized vendors of such imported snacks as hot dogs, potato chips, and popcorn, which they hawk from the tailgates of minivans. But the yatai can still hold their own at night, for in the dark they offer nourishment for soul as well as body.

A single lantern casts a warm, friendly glow on the small circle of faces gathered around the table. There is the savory odor of food and saké, and the sound of animated conversation or laughter, or occasionally of inebriated singing. The customers are certain to be strangers to each other, offering an unparalleled opportunity to speak frankly on any topic, or to favor a well-oiled captive audience with a melancholy song. Then there is the vendor, sure to be a genial host and a sympathetic listener to tales of personal woe. All of this adds up to an irresistible invitation to passers-by in the lonely night—to tired commuters on their way home, to young dandies en route to or from assignations, or to anyone out for a stroll to ponder the problems of the coming day. The yatai are still dear to the hearts of Japanese night owls and are here to stay—at least for a little while longer.

Walter Nichols

Hokōsha-tengoku, 歩行者天国

Pedestrian promenades (literally, "pedestrians' paradise").

During the past decade a new phenomenon has appeared in this land of economic (or, as they are now called, "workaholic") animals. It proves they aren't so economic after all, but endowed no less with reason than with the ability to enjoy life as human beings. For it belongs to reason not only, as Shakespeare says, to look before and after, but also to enjoy life without worrying too much about before and after, or about right and left.

Nowadays on Sundays and holidays amid the crowded streets of Tokyo and the other cities of Japan one comes across sudden oases of peace where one least expects to find them—in the heart of Shinjuku, Shibuya, and Ikebukuro, and along the Ginza. On these days no wheeled vehicle is admitted into these areas, and

pedestrians may stroll along the middle of the road just as they please without fear of being run over—they may only be bumped into by other pedestrians. These are the *hokōsha-tengoku*—or "pedestrians' malls," as they are called in the more pedestrian English phrase.

At such times the Japanese are free to be themselves again, and are no longer the economic animals they seem to be in the wondering eyes of Westerners. The streets, too, are transformed from noisy, crowded thoroughfares into something like the *sandō*, those avenues in front of Shinto shrines, lined with stalls on either side for festivals. Then also the atmosphere is for a precious day or two purified of the polluting smog and filled with a sense of fiesta.

When Minobe Ryōkichi, then governor of Tokyo, introduced this custom he was merely copying something that had already been realized in New York under the administration of Mayor Lindsay. But we should not be too quick to censure the lack of originality, especially when it is a question of recognizing a good idea and putting it into practice. It belongs to the essence of the Japanese character to borrow from other countries; and it is paradoxically by means of such imitation that they assert their national identity and even originality. Nor is this all. While imitating what they find abroad, they invariably introduce subtle changes that improve and extend it in unforeseen ways. This is particularly true of the hokōsha-tengoku. What is for Westerners merely a "mall" is transformed by the Japanese into a veritable "paradise." This is partly by reason of the sudden contrast: where crowds of busy people had been restricted to sidewalks, now the whole street and the people in it are liberated. The resulting atmosphere takes on the character not only of secular enjoyment but also of something approaching religious celebration—though there may be no clearly religious object. One has the feeling that the real roots of this custom are to be traced not to the "secular city" of New York but to the sacred traditions of old Japan. *Plus ça change, plus c'est la même chose.* The more the Japanese seem to lose themselves by following others, the more they find themselves.

Peter Milward

Akadenwa, 赤電話

Public telephones.

Though it is not without cause that Japan has gained the unenviable reputation as one of the most expensive places on earth, there are still a few remaining bargains to be enjoyed, and the public telephone, or *akadenwa,* is one of them. From the standpoint of price, availability, and reliability, the Japanese public-telephone system is second to none. For several decades now the price of a single call has gone unchanged: ¥10 (about 5¢) for the first three minutes of a local call, and ¥10 for each additional three minutes. Finding a phone is rarely a problem—they're everywhere. While Japan ranks seventh in the world in the ratio of private phones to population, it has to be right near the top in the number of public phones. Just in the immediate area surrounding the west entrance of Tokyo's Shinjuku Station, for example, there are no fewer than 250 units. What is even more surprising to the foreigner, they work. Ranking first in equipment and line replacement, Japan can boast the fewest breakdowns and a high level of public confidence in the telephone system.

There are four kinds of public telephones, each with a different use and color. The oldest and most common is the red phone, which has since become the generic term for the public telephone. In general these are used for local calls, and can be found around shops and railway stations. The blue phone allows for both local and long-distance calls and is often located in a phone booth. The yellow phone, also used in phone booths, has the added advantage of accepting ¥100 coins, which is convenient for long-distance conversations. Finally, the pink phones, found in coffee shops and restaurants, are similar to the blue except that they have call-back numbers.

In spite of its good points, however, the system has its minor irritations. Except for the phone booth, most public phones are lined up in an open bank, which makes private conversations something of a chore. Furthermore, the scarcity of coin-changing machines (that they exist at all tends to spoil the foreigner into expecting even more) causes occasional difficulties in using units that accept only ¥10 coins. Especially perturbing, though, is the way that the small number of yellow phones can be monopolized by long lines of young people, especially on weekends, talking to their friends for hours about all those things they don't want to risk being overheard by their parents. For someone in a hurry to make a long-distance connection the inconvenience is obvious.

For all that, the overall performance of the public-telephone system in Japan is something of a technological marvel, which many countries could learn from.

Thomas J. Cogan

Shōsha, 商社

General trading companies.

In this year of 1979, to say that "the sun never sets on Mitsui & Co." would be a fair statement concerning one of Japan's most flourishing *sōgō shōsha.* With its 130 foreign branch offices, its network of telex printers pouring forth a torrent of messages, from the trivial to the world-shaking, around the clock (about fifty thousand a day, to be precise), its thirteen thousand white-collar workers in their shirt sleeves in São Paulo and their drab suits in Tokyo, the total area of competence is almost unlimited. It owns and operates shipping lines, mines copper in Peru and bauxite in Australia, explores for oil in off-shore drilling, imports just about anything that the voracious industrial machinery of

Japan might need, and just as eagerly sells Japanese products abroad. And, in order to circumvent tariff barriers, Mitsui has set up some sixty affiliated companies—especially in the developing countries—whose Japanese executives manage everything from mining ventures to agricultural plantations and fertilizer plants.

The total volume of transactions of the Big Five general trading companies—Mitsubishi, Mitsui, Itō Chū, Marubeni, and Sumitomo —comprises as much as twenty-five percent of the total GNP of Japan. The sales volume of the first two has already exceeded the $100 billion mark. Little wonder that Japan's exports thrive to the tune of complaints from around the world demanding a balance in trade surpluses. Indeed, these gargantuan sōgō shōsha are the secret of Japan's trade success, for they are able to gather and analyze market information and political trends firsthand, to sort things out and project trends, and to keep not only Japanese industry but the government, as well, informed of the state of the world economy. At the same time, they are fully a part of the general cultural system of Japan, where lifelong employment, a loyal spirit of familylike cohesion, and a group-oriented competition are prerequisites. In Western individual-oriented cultures these companies would stand little chance of survival—like the bamboo, which, for all its admirable qualities, simply will not grow in downtown New York.

Intense competition among the top shōsha within Japan, and enormous profits to be gained from government contracts for nuclear power stations, airplane imports, and the like, require a careful lubrication of customer relations through lavish parties and presents. But when government officials are involved in obvious bribery, the public reacts with a vengeance, while the sophisticated shrug and the legion of graduates of top universities continues to line up, unperturbed, to take the entrance exam for the scandal-ridden companies. Outcries come and go, but the sōgō shōsha will stay, a challenge to the ambitions of youth, an organizing force for Japan's exports and imports, and a lighthouse to guide the economy through troubled waters in a difficult and critical world economy.

Johannes Hirschmeier

Depaato, デパート

Department stores.

Faithful to the words of Napoleon, *"La France est un pays de boutiquier,"* the Parisians still do their important shopping at boutiques. For them the very joy of shopping consists in strolling down main street, eyeing the store windows one by one. From start to finish it is the small boutique that is the focus of attention; and the thought that there could be anything enjoyable about shopping in a department store never once crosses the mind. For the Japanese, however, the *depaato* is a place for relaxation, a place to bring the whole family, a place where one gets friendly, quality service—anything but just another boring building in which to shop.

I can still recall my impressions upon stepping into a Japanese department store for the first time fifteen years ago: the polite bow and high-pitched *"irasshaimase"* ("welcome") of the white-gloved girl greeting me at the escalator and wiping the dust from the hand railing with a dainty cloth. How particular these people are about cleanliness, I remember thinking to myself.

The depaato is pure service: the carefully drilled alertness to detail of the employees, the magical skill and beauty of the way they wrap their packages, the free delivery service anywhere in the city—even a half dozen handkerchiefs or a simple blouse purchased as a gift for a friend will be forwarded on for you. During the gift-exchanging seasons of July and December a special department is opened up with its own consultant to aid you with your purchases. During the warmer months the tired shopper can always rest in the rooftop garden while the children romp about in the playground there. And a special floor provides the hungry shopper with a whole row of restaurants to choose from, specializing in everything from Japanese and Chinese cuisine to German, Italian, and French. There are strollers for the kids and, if you look around, even department stores with free nursery service.

But the most impressive thing of all is the assortment of cultural activities that take place at the depaato. On the entertainment floor, tastefully designed exhibitions of temple treasures, ancient works of art, swords, pottery, woodblock prints, and Japanese and foreign paintings are displayed regularly one after another. These mini art museums are either free of charge or require only a minimal entrance fee, and one can consult the newspaper for a complete listing of what shows are available to choose from. This kind of service may be meant to encourage sales, but I appreciate the keen sensitivity to cultural life that the Japanese depaato shows and the importance of the contribution it makes.

The depaato is a mirror of society. Anyone who enters it will be quick to understand the prosperity, the cosmopolitanism, and the service quality that are very much a part of Japan. One can only hope that the menacing winds of time and economics will pass the depaato by and let it remain just as it is.

Françoise Moréchand

Shataku, 社宅

Company housing.

Occasional newspaper stories confirm what those living here already know: that Tokyo is in many respects the most expensive city in the world. Given the high population density, it is no surprise that housing should be high-priced as well. Glancing at one of Tokyo's English-language dailies, one finds two-room apartments going for $1,000 a month, small houses with no gardens for $3,000, and so forth.

What's a poor fellow to do? His options come down to these: he may inherit a house from somebody; he can get lucky in the lottery for the relatively cheap government apartments; he can rent a couple of rooms in one of the seedy buildings in areas not fancy enough for the English-language classifieds; or he can borrow a fantastic sum to buy a house or condominium apartment, and then spend two decades paying for it while most likely having to commute an hour and a half or more each way to work. But if he has the good fortune or foresight to work for one of the well-established companies that provide housing for their employees, he can live at a moderate expense within an hour or less of his office. This is not a permanent solution, since there seems to be an unwritten rule that the employee will move out by the age of forty or forty-five, but at least the rent he has saved in the meantime will help with the down payment on a place of his own.

Along with annual bonuses of several months' salary, family allowances, seasonal resorts at reduced prices, subsidies for social clubs, and the like, company housing has become a necessity for large companies that hope to attract the talent they need. At the same time, it enables the company to shift its employees to out-of-the-way sites without having to face the complaints of leaving them stranded without lodgings.

Many Japanese companies have bachelor dormitories, or *ryō,* but the term *shataku* is commonly reserved for the housing provided for families in buildings owned or rented by the company. Inside, the apartment will usually consist of a kitchen, bath, and

two or three tatami rooms—by Japanese standards an adequate space for a family of four. Around the building there may be the luxury of some green space, play areas for the children, storage sheds, and even the occasional parking lot (particularly welcome in Tokyo, where off-street parking places are rented at handsome monthly rates).

Many Westerners would probably be leery of the very thought of company housing and all the imagery of paternalistic employers that goes along with it. But the slight loss of privacy is more than offset, at least in my own case, by the benefit of knowing my neighbors and having a sense of community with them. And for the Japanese, it is an easy, if temporary, solution to the perennial problem of keeping a roof over the head.

Jeremy Whipple

Nōkyō, 農協

Agricultural cooperatives.

It is not uncommon these days to see a group of sun-darkened Japanese farmers, neatly dressed in old-fashioned Western suits, traveling together on a sightseeing tour to someplace in Japan or abroad. The image of the poor farmer bound to his fields is thus fast becoming a thing of the past, thanks both to the increased value of land and to the efficiency of local agricultural cooperatives, or *nōkyō*.

Agricultural cooperative-societies were established across Japan during the land reforms that followed World War II. The system of tenant farming controlled by landlords was abolished, and the large estates were parceled out in small sections of from ten to twenty acres to the new owner-farmer. Today virtually every farm household belongs to one of the over ten thousand cooperatives with a combined membership of nearly six million regular members. In addition to both purchasing fertilizer, seed, and equipment in bulk and coordinating marketing, the cooperatives also provide extensive credit and other banking services. Most also support a variety of community associations and maintain close ties with prefectural and national federations. The Central Union, representing the nōkyō on a national level, operates several different programs and is active politically. The Farmers' Cooperative Bank (Nōrin Chūkin) has assets of several billion dollars.

Despite the efforts of the cooperatives to improve the status of farmers, they are often still portrayed on television as entertaining bumpkins whose rough dialect and naiveté provide a rich mine for situation comedies. But this picture is quite unfair. In many ways the farmers are closer to the heart of Japanese culture than their brothers in the city.

I remember visiting a most interesting agricultural high school in Ibaraki Prefecture. Noted for its modern methods and its active support of the nōkyō, the school had managed to combine the best of technology with the best of the traditional Japanese spirit. *Zazen* meditation was regularly scheduled; there were training sessions in judo and swordsmanship, as well as lectures on the Japanese and Chinese classics. Several of the teachers, well into their seventies, were equally adept with hoe, sword, and brush. In an austere but lively way, such schools are preserving the rich and many-faceted heritage of the farmer.

Another important aspect of the farmer's life is folkcrafts. Producing fine textiles, wooden bowls, baskets, and delicate needlework, a number of Japan's "living national treasures" are farmers who still work the fields. Some cooperatives are making efforts to support these crafts, without which Japan would be incalculably impoverished.

Can it be an accident, then, that so many of the key words of Japanese poetry—*fūryū* (refinement), *shibui* (austere simplicity), *wabi* (poverty), *sabi* (solitude)—all express rural values?

The beginning of culture:
Rice-planting songs
Deep in the country. —Bashō

John Stevens

Jieitai, 自衛隊

The national defense forces.

Even the observant visitor to Japan needs a sharp eye to notice that the country has any defense force at all. Sometimes, on the crowded express trains coming up to Tokyo from Yokosuka on Tokyo Bay, you can see well-behaved young men dressed in smart, but unfamiliar navy uniforms. The Yokosuka Naval Base itself, the oldest in Japan, at first looks to be exuberantly all-American; but if you look closely you can generally see one or two destroyers of the Maritime Self-Defense Force, a different shade of camouflage gray, flying the Japanese naval ensign, a rising sun with radiating red rays. Even less frequently will you see a low-flying military plane or a helicopter with that unmistakable large red dot. Around the area of Mount Fuji and on the back roads of Hokkaido, Japan's relatively less populated northern island, you may occa-

sionally run across a jeep full of soldiers in steel helmets, marked with a white cherry blossom. And once in a blue moon you might get a distant glimpse of a dark green tank on maneuvers.

Yet this is all the average Japanese sees of his defense forces, too. Military parades are all but unknown, exercises take place far away from civilians, and the Japanese press carries few reports of Self-Defense Force activities. When they do, they are almost always stories of help given by SDF units after floods and earthquakes.

The postwar Japanese constitution explicitly renounces war—which has been interpreted to mean that only a minimum force suitable for the defense of the Japanese home islands should be maintained. The Japanese government has followed this principle by keeping defense spending below one percent of the Gross National Product, by far the lowest proportion of any industrialized country. The entire SDF numbers only about 260,000 men and women. Civilian control of the military is strictly enforced, with the prime minister of Japan as the commander-in-chief.

For several years after the war, the existence of even a small self-defense force was a matter of public debate. Bitter memories of Japan's sufferings under military rule, the protection offered to Japan by the Mutual Security Treaty with the United States, and the impossibility of Japan's defending her worldwide trade routes by herself combined to make many Japanese feel that military forces of her own were both dangerous and unnecessary. That feeling has changed to the point that the majority of Japanese now accept the idea that their country should have its own defense forces, like every other country in the world.

But the policy of "defense only" remains as popular as ever. It has brought not only peace, but the greatest prosperity Japan has ever known. To most Japanese, any return to the unhappy years of military rule is unthinkable, and the best way to prevent this is to keep the country's military forces small, low in profile, and under the control of the civilian government. The members of the SDF seem to accept this view of themselves, which may be one reason why they are, in my experience, among the politest, best-behaved, and least conspicuous military people in the world.

Murray Sayle

Tōdai, 東大
Tokyo University.

One summer's day, walking down the streets of Tokyo, I was stopped short by a policeman. For what reason I cannot say, he sternly demanded my Certificate of Alien Registration. Obediently, I opened my wallet and out it fell, together with my student I. D. Before I even had time to hand him what he wanted, the policeman, who had been watching me carefully, stepped back, drew himself up to attention, saluted, announced, *"Shitsurei shimashita"* ("I beg your pardon"), and departed.

What he had seen that changed his whole demeanor from one of authoritarianism to embarrassment was that little card that identified me as a student engaged in research at the prestigious Tokyo University—that little "passport to heaven" that offers a way into society for a few select Japanese and gives the foreigner the added advantage of a practical detour around much of the usual red tape.

The history of Tōkyō Daigaku (usually abbreviated as Tōdai) is not very long by Japan's standards. Though its roots can be traced back to the educational system of the Tokugawa shogunate, the official date of its foundation as a state institution is 1877. Given Japan's emphasis on political values and the concentration of political power in Tokyo, it was perhaps inevitable that such state universities should become subject to government influence. In Tōdai's early years, for example, a whole array of foreign teachers was hired to put the new scholarly and political community on the right track. And with equal efficiency, they were dismissed when that imperial university had grown capable of managing its own affairs.

All questions of government involvement aside, when the students of Japan were caught up in the general current of anti-establishment protest in the late 1960s and succeeded in making Tōdai their last bastion, the whole uprising ended in a tragicomic battle for the defense of the university's ransacked Yasuda Hall: hordes of students weeping from the gas bombs and dripping wet from the hoses that had been used against them, surrendering to

the riot police—leaving the people of Japan to wonder which side best embodied the traditional samurai spirit.

In the same pragmatic way that the Japanese so often respond to controls from above, they look up to Tōdai as the pinnacle of learning, but not as an impregnable fortress. A simple country boy with brains in his head and determination in his heart can earn admission, graduate, and acquire a high rank in society. And, should he come from Tōdai's prestigious Law Department, he can even become prime minister. (Nine of the fourteen postwar heads of state have been graduates of Tōdai.) So don't be surprised when you chance to overhear elementary-school children discussing which prep school will bring them most safely to the gates of Tokyo University. Perhaps in the next generation, even the kindergarten children will be bothered with this everyday problem. Many of their mammas already are.

Jan Swyngedouw

Juku, 塾

Private supplementary schools.

Jun-chan used to drop over of an afternoon to play with the dog and practice pitching against our garden wall. He was in the sixth grade. When he stopped coming, I guessed he had begun to attend a *juku* of some sort after regular school hours. Come spring vacation he appeared again, mit and ball in hand, and told me how three times a week he had been walking to a nearby juku that offers special help in mathematics, language, and social studies. On Sundays he commuted to a downtown Tokyo *shingaku-juku,* or cram school, there to test himself against two thousand other pupils also competing for the entrance examination to those prestigious high schools that are the springboards to success in Japanese society. Jun-chan looked tired and had gained weight. His pitching was awful.

For a bright child like Jun-chan, public schools do not offer enough challenge. His parents knew that for the best education he would need more and so decided to enroll him in the small-scale, flexible classroom situation of the juku, where he could get that extra edge. Invariably privately run, juku classes may be held anywhere, from a tatami room in a private home to a dusky, rented apartment under the tracks, vacant university classrooms on weekends, or the halls of longstanding, incorporated juku of national fame. Some juku are faithful to the principles of traditional education; others take the opportunity in remedial teaching to try out methods that would be considered heretical in public education. But their most important quality is that they provide individual-centered training for pupils who may be bored or left behind by public school. Since Japanese education is controlled centrally by the Ministry of Education and citizens have little say in the system, juku provide parents some measure of choice in their children's education.

Juku have increased in number so rapidly over the last decade that this has been called the *ranjuku jidai,* "the age of madly proliferating juku." In 1977 there were no less than fifty thousand of them scattered throughout the country, more than sixty percent of these founded after 1966. The sons and daughters of Japan's upwardly mobile population commute distances from half a mile to halfway across the islands to seek the educational services the juku render.

With juku added to an already heavy study load, a child may have little energy left for other things; and the narrowness this produces has brought the juku under heavy fire. As some critics argue, moreover, statistics show that all the money given to extra classes and the efforts made to ensure graduation from a prestigious school really do not guarantee one's chances of success in modern Japanese society. But all that aside, as long as the myth survives among parents that their children's future depends on the amount of schooling they undergo, and as long as children continue to show that typical aversion to being left out of what "everyone else is doing," there is little chance of the juku losing its present importance.

Lynne E. Riggs

Omawari-san, お巡りさん

The patrolman (the *san* here is an honorific).

Nowadays the very word "policeman" conjures up images of violence and corruption. These may be the occupational hazards of any police system, and the way the mass media tends to overreact is no doubt part of it, too. But I must say, from my own experience, that the Japanese *omawari-san,* or patrolman, belongs to another class altogether and that his image affects the common attitude toward police in general.

I remember once rushing out of the hospital where I worked, hopping on to my old wreck of a motorbike, and flying out into

the street in gallant aplomb. "Hey, where do you think you're going?" By the time it registered that the words were meant for me, I realized that, in my haste, I had set out the wrong way on a one-way street. And with that the officer promptly hauled me off to a local police box, sat me down, and prepared to book me. "So sorry, so sorry," I kept repeating–knowing full well that I had no excuse, but the words took effect. Pen poised in midair, he looked at me, leaned back in his chair, and broke into a gentle, fatherly lecture on the rules of the road. In no time we were around to small talk and I knew he was going to let me off. "You take care from now on, eh." He finally dismissed me. And the words stuck with me.

To say I got special treatment because I am a foreigner would be to miss the point. Mine was a common experience in Japan, where conditions are different from what they are abroad. In the first place, when police fire questions that seem to have no relationship to the matter at hand, the foreigner feels irate at the invasion of privacy. But in Japan, the gathering of background by the police is taken as a sign of kindness and concern. Second, booking is coldly mechanical in other countries, and court orders are perfunctorily issued when fees cannot be paid on the spot. The mood is irritating, and one tends to brace oneself to fight for one's rights. In Japan there is a good deal more humanity about it all, which rather takes the foreigner by surprise.

When I first applied for my driver's license in Japan, I was sent to the police station for a lecture as part of the procedure. I remember taking my seat with the same queasy feeling I used to get at such places back in Australia, totally unprepared for what actually took place. Addressing the assembly in a warm, human tone, accented by a delightful Okayama dialect, the officer in charge lectured on the law and the social effects of accidents. Heads nodding obediently, the audience hung on his every word, in a spirit of harmony that seemed to erase all barriers and to absorb his concerns into their own. That image imprinted on my memory, I have often thought one of the things that makes daily life in Japan so smooth is that there is so little friction between the police and the people.

Alan Talbot

Koseki, 戸籍

The official family register.

The *koseki* is the premier emblem of official identity in Japan. No Japanese citizen is without one. Indeed, two major requirements for any naturalized citizen are adoption of a Japanese name and establishment of a family register, even though it may comprise a family of one.

Like most things in life, the koseki can be both a burden and a blessing. Among its best-known drawbacks is that it may be examined by prospective parents-in-law or employers eager to pry into one's family background. Any "flaws" perceived can put an end to one's hopes and ambitions. For instance, record of belonging to the so-called *buraku*—Japan's former outcaste group against which considerable prejudice still prevails—will be so indicated.

On the other hand, a koseki, copies of which are easily obtained for a nominal fee from one's local registry office, can be a very handy thing to have. For one thing, such a copy is accepted anywhere as irrefutable evidence of one's identity, even though no photograph is attached, so ingrained is the respect for the family register.

A peculiar feature of the koseki, to the non-Japanese at least, is that one's family home may be listed as a place one has never lived. This is so because it is a *family* register, not merely an individual identity badge. Thus, an unmarried person is usually included on the parents' koseki, so that it is their address that appears on the children's official documents, such as passports.

Which brings me to another feature of the koseki, and one that well illustrates its central importance in determining one's public identity. The only legal requirement for marriage in Japan is the establishment of a new, joint koseki, which can be accomplished with no trouble at one's local registry. Do this, and you are wedded in the eyes of the state. Omit it, and no matter how many ceremonies have been celebrated, you are simply living together. Either spouse may assume the family name of the other. That is,

a man may marry into a woman's family, as is often done when the wife's family has no male heir.

A great deal has been written about the lessening importance of the family system in Japan. Yet in spite of the many social changes since the war and the proliferation of the nuclear family, the family register clearly remains the basis of the individual's legal and social persona.

Suzanne Trumbull

Kamon, 家紋

Family crests.

The problem of effectively reducing visual expression to the very minimum has long been the concern of the artist. But perhaps nowhere in the history of the past thousand years can examples of this process of simplification be found to equal those seen in the Japanese crest. No wonder the history and development of the symbolism of these remarkable patterns have been the subject of such fascinating and thoroughgoing research.

The crest originated from the need to identify friend from foe in the days of hand-to-hand combat—much as flags and banners were used in the West. When the crest was later adopted as a family symbol, however, variations arose that would create thousands upon thousands of unique designs. That these numerous abstracted symbols could easily be distinguished one from another attests to a high level of culture that not only loved and appreciated the things of nature but was sensitive to minute differences in her patterns. (Most of us are aware, for instance, that there are many five-petaled blossoms in the botanical world, but how many of us would know that the *notched* five-petaled flower is common to but one species?) The designer of a crest had to simplify his subject graphically, selecting characteristics that would be both accurate and unlikely to be confused.

Superimposed on this exacting visual knowledge was a more involved intellectual system that attributed abstract characteristics to the subject through historical, poetic, or literary allusions. Some related to ancient China; others had more mythological roots. But whatever the case, the whole lexicon of imagery was a matter of common appreciation and most assuredly entered into the choice of subject for a crest.

The coupling of these attributes grew into an esoteric art of its own in time, drawing on an ever wider assortment of concepts and historical references. Even the pun played an important part in cases where the double meaning carried an auspicious meaning. For instance, the word *masu,* which meant a conventional square wooden box in standard graduated sizes used as a measure for rice, conveyed the additional meaning "to prosper" or "to increase," thus suggesting a number of visual patterns. Pine needles, which grow in pairs and remain attached even after falling, suggested marital fidelity, as did the monogamous Mandarin duck, which even today is much in evidence in the decor at weddings.

Western influences have exercised vast changes in the traditional life style of the Japanese, including the substitution of simpler dress for the kimono and less frequent use of the family crest. Although the kimono is not part of the wardrobes of nisei and sansei living abroad, the knowledge and significance of their own family crests is still proudly preserved. Surely the charmingly simple family crest itself will survive in Japan.

Frances Blakemore

Ofukuro, おふくろ

Mom; Ma.

One aspect of Japanese society that often arouses Western consternation is the family system. And no aspect of the system is more striking than the relationship between mother and son. Sons commonly refer to their mothers as *ofukuro* in situations where Americans might say "my mom." The origin of the term is obscure, opinion being divided as to whether it is based on an old name for womb or a contraction of the word for bosom. But whichever interpretation you choose, it is clear that the term, used by Japanese men throughout their lives, connotes a deep emotional tie to the mother. Its use suggests, however unconsciously,

the protective role of the mother and the correspondingly dependent role of the son.

Japanese men are hardly furtive about this relationship, especially when they are young. Not infrequently mothers accompany their sons to the big city for college entrance examinations. A young man apartment hunting for the first time will often leave the choice to his mother—even if he is married. College graduates preparing to enter a company swarm into department stores in early spring to buy a suit for their new job—with mother in tow to have the final say. All this is done with an aplomb that confounds more independent-minded Westerners.

Older, married men are less visibly dependent on their mothers, but the attitude remains and is the basis for the tendency of Japanese men to view their wives less as partners in marriage than as surrogate mothers—and to seek outside the home the kind of relationship Western men expect with their wives. If anyone has the right to complain about the situation it is the wives, yet even today they remain remarkably quiet about it all. Instead, they focus their emotional energies on their children, especially their sons. Thus, the pattern is repeated.

In the last two decades, increased affluence and smaller family size have allowed Japanese mothers, always primarily family-oriented, to devote even more attention to their children; and the degree to which young men depend on their mothers seems greater than ever. Some Japanese critics have seen in this a "mother complex" among Japanese males; but it has none of the Oedipal overtones it might have in the West, suggesting instead an undue reliance on one's mother and a tendency to form mother-son relationships with women in general. Yet I wonder if this is true, or whether it is not the mother who is more dependent on her children.

Other factors work against this bond; the cramped quarters of Japan's major cities, for example, make it increasingly impractical, if not impossible, for sons to live near their parents. Still, the ties do seem to persist and, whatever their baleful influence, do not seem to have shaken the stability of family life in Japan—something an American can only look on with envy.

Stephen W. McCallion

Senpai, 先輩

One's senior in school or at work.

Senpai is one of those words that Westerners living in Japan find hard to keep out of conversations in their native tongue for the simple reason that they have no equivalent. "I had dinner with a senpai of mine last night," comes out much more smoothly than if one had referred to "someone who preceded me at school (or at work)" or to the confusing term "senior."

Expedient though the word may be to Westerners, their use only partially reflects what senpai actually means to the Japanese themselves. True, they use it generically to indicate those who have entered a school, a company, or the like before them, and who therefore are accorded a certain deference not given peers or juniors. But in practice, and in its most meaningful sense, senpai is used more selectively in reference to one person—or at most a few persons—who acts as one's guide and mentor. The relationship here is based first on seniority and status, but this frequently develops into close ties where the senpai may function as confidant, financial advisor, and even matchmaker to his *kōhai,* or junior.

Such relationships are generally formed in college, but since one's loyalties and interests are ultimately focused on one's place of work, it is the senpai on the job who is more likely to play a strong role in one's life. And since women rarely remain very long on a job, even if they want to, the deepest senpai-kōhai ties are found among men. When a man enters a job, someone will act as a senpai of sorts, breaking him in and teaching him the ropes. Often this association evolves into a personal one, but not always; if the right "feeling" is not there, the young man will look elsewhere in the company for the guidance and friendship he needs. In any case, a senpai will assume the role of benefactor, taking the kōhai under wing, advising him, treating him to drinks after work, and in general trying to make life easier for him. Once established, the senpai-kōhai relationship will almost never be forgotten, regardless of changes in formal status or position. Even old age does not affect it; once a senpai, always a senpai.

Since Japan opened its doors to the West in the nineteenth century the Japanese have accepted capitalism with a fervor that would make robber barons blush. But as with so many Western imports, they have added their own elements to reduce tensions and to protect their social structures. The senpai-kōhai relationship is one such element, serving to soften an atmosphere that might otherwise be intolerably competitive. Essentially hierarchical, the relationship nonetheless is one in which superiority carries with it a set of obligations as well as a set of perquisites, and one where friendship often humanizes the distinctions involved.

Stephen W. McCallion

酔っ払えば都
A DRUNKS PARADISE IS HERE

Yopparai
酔払い
Inebriation.

In 1956, a judge of the Kyoto District Court acquitted a man of attempted murder because he, the would-be murderer, was drunk. The judge—a maverick—was trying to call forth criticism of what he thought was a bad statute on the books: "No punishment shall be meted out to anyone who commits a crime after the loss of mental soundness due to heavy drink."

The judge's cynical ruling did not produce the kind of response he sought. Instead of outrage, the public picked up the ambiguous phrase he coined in lamenting that Japan was a "paradise for drunks" (*yopparai no tengoku*) and used it in an approving sense.

A year later, another judge, in the Tokyo District Court, took the opposite tack to challenge the "paradise for drunks" statute. To a man who had caused an accident while driving a car under the influence of alcohol, he handed down an unprecedentedly severe jail sentence. Now, inconsistent as it may appear, this justice also met with wide public acclaim.

That may have been due to the fact that the public was just then becoming aroused over the rapidly increasing traffic, which was making the streets unsafe. The driver won no sympathy at all. But there may have been another factor—he had, after all, plowed his car into a *yatai,* or nighttime street stall, where some people were enjoying their food and drink.

From that there followed a step-by-step process whereby the Japanese developed a consummate intolerance of drunken driving, or *yopparai unten.* Today it is the ultimate offense, bringing instant confiscation of the driver's license whether there's been an accident or not. Worse, drunkenness is defined with amazing simplicity as any trace whatsoever of alcohol in the blood. One hears no complaining of these Draconian rules; all Japan has decided firmly against drunken driving.

Yet this same Japan continues to adore its drunks (*yopparai*). There is no contradiction here. The drunken driver is a modern manifestation who bears no relationship to the other, whereas the Japanese drunk is a veritable national treasure. Traditionally this ubiquitous figure has been the object of love, envy, amusement, compassion, and—yes—respect.

But isn't this changing nowadays? Not really. The challenge of the 50s has been neatly resolved with the elimination of the inebriation-alibi statute (which doesn't mean the principle can't be followed when desired) and the setting up of a special category for the drunken driver. This preserves the status of the yopparai.

Popular drama, now on television, still abounds in examples of the sympathetic drunk, just as centuries ago, the Japanese saw the drunk as being in temporary escape from this painful world; one would no more reprimand him than one would an angel.

Japanese drunks, like most others, tend to be boisterous and annoying to sober people, but their cheerful way of drinking is offered by a Japanese psychiatrist as one reason there aren't many alcoholics. It stands to reason. After all, this society produced that unique image of the drunk, which is still cherished—so much so that when Japanese get drunk they behave as though they had something to live up to. As they do.

Holloway Brown

Minoue Sōdan, 身上相談

Personal advice.

The scene is standard: a bowl of flowers or a translucent screen provides for a gently sobbing figure some anonymity from the TV cameras; a panel of "experts" in human affairs sits out in front waiting to give advice.

Only the story varies. Today it is that of an attractive middle-class woman whose older husband has found out about her affair

with a younger man. Yesterday it was that of an office girl, pregnant and abandoned by her boyfriend. Tomorrow it will be that of a housewife who has fallen among loan sharks. After that, who knows. But one thing is certain: that uniquely Japanese institution the *minoue sōdan* (literally, "discussions of a personal nature") will endure well into the future.

For the average outsider, the whole thing is a mystery. The Japanese, we are told, are highly sensitive to shame and public exposure. Yet here we have a constant parade of troubled humanity, mostly female, willing to bare its most intimate problems and seek public advice. And these people do so without any of the Western guilt feelings about adultery, abortion, and so on.

Perhaps it is the Japanese answer to our confessional box.

Be that as it may, for students of Japan the minoue sōdan is a gold mine. One "discussion" alone will run for the best part of an hour, complete with charts and diagrams showing who is related to whom, who has been betrayed by whom, and so on. Often there will be live and very realistic enactments of the crucial scenes in the saga, the seductions in particular. Spread out before you are the complex mores of what is supposed to be a closed society.

The newspapers and magazines also have their minoue sōdan columns, with equally frank detail.

The advice given is just as revealing: mostly conservative and male-oriented, with the woman urged to make one more effort to forgive her husband's affairs, drunkenness, or what have you. A new generation of female "experts" is trying to change things, but like most things social in Japan it will take time.

Gregory Clark

Hesokuri, へそくり

The "sugar bowl"; a private purse.

In reading through the whimsical *senryū* poems of eighteenth-century Japan we run across the phrase, used of a young man in need of spending money, that he was "pining for his mother's navel." The expression has nothing at all to do with "still being tied to the umbilical cord." It refers rather to that precious space between the kimono and the obi, waist high, where mother kept her private purse. Like the sugar bowl and the cookie jar in the West, the *hesokuri* (literally, "navel savings") was a fund that a woman kept carefully hidden from her husband and used for her own needs or that of her children.

Stories dating from the Edo period tell of mothers taking pity on the financial state of their prodigal sons, dipping into the hesokuri, and issuing the warning, "Now keep this from your father." Their anxiety was not without cause, for if found out, they would get into serious trouble and perhaps even be divorced.

In our own day, however, the tables are frequently turned so that it is the husband who must keep the hesokuri. In Japan, eight out of ten men paid a monthly salary hand over their pay envelopes, without breaking the seal, to their wives. It is the woman who manages household finances, and to whom the man must turn for his pocket money. And so, with fear and trembling, he stealthily contrives to set aside an emergency fund to support his entertainments and leave him enough for the all-important saké.

In France, perhaps as a reaction to hard times, a number of people have taken interest in reading the adventures of a certain famous detective. The hero is a dauntless, courageous officer of the law who crushes foreign spies like insects and is not afraid to punch up his superiors from time to time. But there is an Achilles' heel in this free and independent spirit. Returning home with his overtime pay in hand he is confronted with the eternal problem of how to swindle his wife out of a little extra spending money. Ravishing his trousers and desk drawers with the skills of a professional spy, she drives him to the brink of despair. Exacting from the government the pledge to guard his latest raise as top secret, he employs a computer to devise a scheme to secure him a little cash for his private frivolities. But the computer is no match for his wife.

The situation is much the same in Japan where, as the saying goes, "the things that hold up most firmly since the war are women and socks." If our poor detective would come here he would find a country in which the man's authority has gone downhill in inverse proportion to the rise in income and national growth. But perhaps, out of the rich experience accumulated by the community of husbands united in the effort to cheat their wives out of an extra yen or two, he might learn a trick or two to take home to France.

Jacques Thiriet

Hirōen, 披露宴

A wedding reception.

To the Westerner used to wedding receptions that are supposed to evolve from initial formalities into a semiformal carousal complete with practical jokes on the newlyweds, the Japanese *hirōen* seems an altogether stiff and staid affair, too boring to merit the name of a celebration. It may seem that way to a lot of Japanese, too, but as long as the fundamental structures of matrimony remain what they are in Japan, there is little chance of things changing.

As the ideograms in the name tell us, the hirōen is an "introducing banquet," in which the bride and groom are officially presented to one another's families. Traditionally, the hirōen was held at home, after the wedding ceremony at a local Shinto shrine. But the lack of space in urban dwellings and the new postwar affluence have combined to transform it into a highly formalized, lavish affair, usually held at a *kekkonshikijō,* or wedding hall, which may be decorated in any style from typically Western to typically Japanese.

The guests, fifty or more of them, arrive and sign the register at the reception desk, leaving off at the same time a special brightly decorated envelope with at least a ¥10,000 note inside to help defray the costs of the banquet. The men in their Western suits and the women in their kimonos (this is the usual dress nowadays) are then seen to their assigned seats. At the head table sits the bride and groom, flanked by the matchmaking couple or couples, the *nakōdo*. A Master of Ceremonies announces the order of the day and introduces each speaker, beginning with one of the nakōdo, who in turn introduces the newlyweds in a long speech, detailing their educational and occupational backgrounds. In addition, the speaker is expected to praise the bride as *saien* and the groom as *shūsai* (persons of great ability) and to describe them in terms that the West usually reserves for funeral eulogies. Special guests of the bride and groom, usually persons closely associated with them in their work or from their school days, then rise to give speeches. After a toast, the banquet is served. Sometime during the banquet, the bride slips away to change clothes. This custom, known as the *o-ironaoshi,* or "changing of the colors," usually means exchanging the traditional Japanese wedding dress for Western clothes, although the reverse can also occur. After the banquet, speeches are delivered by representatives of the relatives and friends of the bride and groom. The final speech is given customarily by the father of the groom, thanking the nakōdo and the guests for their cooperation. The M. C. then announces the formal conclusion as the bride and groom, their parents, and the nakōdo see the guests to the door, offering each one a gift box—containing some specially prepared food and a practical gift.

The idea of the bride and groom sneaking off on a secret honeymoon, leaving the guests to party by themselves, would be an affront to the very meaning of the hirōen. And perhaps, too, it shows the fundamental difference in attitude toward marriage that distinguishes Japan from the West.

Richard F. Szippl

Beiju, 米寿

The eighty-eighth birthday.

Beiju, literally, the "age of rice," in Japan denotes one's eighty-eighth birthday. The reference to rice is not to the food but to its Chinese character. Breaking it down like a rebus into three parts, that character, 米, becomes 八十八, which gives the characters for eighty-eight. Similar denotations are used for the seventy-seventh and ninety-ninth birthdays. In cursive style the character for "rejoice," 㐂, gives us the elements 七十七, or seventy-seven, making it the "age of joy," *kiju.* That ninety-nine is called *hakuju,* the "white age," has nothing at all to do with the white hair or bald head of old age but is simply the result of subtracting the character for one, 一, from the character for one hundred, 百, leaving 白, white.

Celebrations for old age begin at sixty. While that may seem rather early to us, it was not so some generations ago. A famous old Japanese proverb has it that "Life lasts only fifty years"; and in China celebrations for old age once started at forty. The sixtieth birthday (or, according to the Japanese way of reckoning, which counts birth as one's first birthday, the sixty-first birthday), or *kanreki,* is given special attention because it is the time when the sexagenarian calendar of East Asia repeats the same combination of signs that marked the year of birth. Hence the sixtieth birthday recalls birth and is seen as a kind of rebirth. Close relations, neighbors, and friends come together to present the initiate into old age with a red headdress and a red vest without sleeves. Traditionally, men of this age were relieved of their duties in the community and could abdicate their role as head of the family. They were called *go-inkyo*—retired masters. Those who could afford it retired even earlier to devote themselves to the pursuit of their own interests—poetry, flowers, music, or whatever—a life called *rakuinkyo,* or pleasant retirement. The movement in contemporary Japan to change the retirement age from fifty-five to sixty should not be seen as a proof of their "workaholism," as is often

said, but simply as a consequence of the need to reform old-age pension schemes.

After sixty, the next great event takes place at age seventy, which is called *koki,* the rare old age. The name goes back to the saying that "A man seldom lives to be seventy," attributed to Tu Fu, the great Chinese poet of the T'ang Dynasty. With the seventy-seventh, eighty-eighth, and ninety-ninth birthdays, then, the cycle of old-age celebrations comes to its end.

With a life expectancy of 72.69 years for men and 77.95 for women, the Japanese are now the longest lived people in the world. To be sure, the rapid aging of society has brought with it its share of problems, requiring greater effort if old age is to become indeed the "age of joy" that it is promised to be.

Sepp Linhart

O-seibo, お歳暮

Year-end gifts.

Every society has its special occasions and seasons for gift giving. In Japan the greatest of these in terms of volume of gifts exchanged is the time of *seibo,* which runs from about December 10 to the end of the month—with the mid-year *chūgen* running a close second. Gifts given at seibo are meant to express gratitude for help or favors received throughout the year. While individual gifts predominate, it is not uncommon for companies to offer seibo to their customers.

In former times the giver was expected to present his gifts in person, and this is still considered the proper thing to do as a way of showing respect for the recipient. The pace of modern life, however, has made it increasingly difficult not only to find the time to make the rounds to distribute gifts, but also to remain at home to entertain those who come bearing presents as well. In the case of those engaged in personal-service occupations, such as doctors, this latter burden would be impossible. Thus it has become the custom nowadays to have seibo delivered through the department stores or the postal service.

As the seibo season approaches, a housewife and her husband consult on whom they should offer seibo to and how much they should spend, but it is the wife in most cases who actually does the shopping. Of course, determining just what gifts to buy "for the man or woman who has everything" is another thing altogether, and usually ends up in something ordinary and unimaginative. Food—especially liquor but even staples like sugar and canned fruits—is the most common seibo, although articles of clothing are not unusual.

In Japan it is not only the value of the gift but the prestige of the store from which it comes that determines the impression made on the recipient. Accordingly, seibo are presented in the clearly marked wrapping paper of the place of purchase—something that would be considered improper if not outright rude in the West. The larger department stores offer special "gift corners" during the seibo season, displaying hundreds of sample gifts prepackaged and ready to deliver, and providing special consultants to aid in the selection.

Not to be outdone, smaller retail shops and speciality stores run sales campaigns of their own, bombarding the public with reminders of their social obligations and competing for a piece of those generous end-of-the-year bonuses that companies present their employees. The giving of gifts in modern Japan has lost much of its spontaneity as a result of all of this—indeed, the number of gifts exchanged is seen as a barometer of social status—and is even considered by many a seasonal nuisance. But as long as most Japanese lack the courage to resist those commercial pressures that prey on their "debts of gratitude," there seems little chance that freedom of expression will be restored to this important and universal way of saying, "Thank you."

Harumi Befu

Onsen, 温泉

Hot springs.

So many things, for one with a theoretical turn of mind, can be made into theories of Japanese culture. Among them is the hot spring.

Since very ancient times physical cleanliness has for the Japanese contained religious elements. Relations between gods and man in the primitive Japanese view of the universe have been easy and uncomplicated. Among the principal things that men must avoid if they are to be on good terms with gods is physical pollution. If by some accident pollution occurs, it must be taken away, and one of the methods of removing it is the most obvious one: to have a good bath.

It is often said that the Japanese are not a religious people. I wonder if this is not a mistake arising from the fact that relations between gods and men continue to be uncomplicated. Many things that are in their way religious, therefore, do not strike us Westerners as such. They are not absolute and inexorable enough. The observances of Shinto are not earnest enough to be acknowledged as religious. The essential element of the religious, the recognition of gods, is present all the same, and so perhaps the Japanese are more religious than the common view has them to be.

There is much of Shinto in the cult of the hot spring. There is the washing, of course, lengthy and repeated, and there is the return to nature. At no European spa is there so much bathing or such intimacy with nature. Many of the most famous Japanese hot springs ran out of natural hot water long ago, and so it is artificially heated, no different, essentially, from an artificially heated bath back at home.

What is different is the setting, the sense of having the mountains not merely there to look at, but to be sunk into. At a European spa there is usually at least a pretense that immersion in the baths is good for the health. In Japan the therapeutic effect is rather on the spirit. One is lazily at ease, and accepts things.

The other day a Japanese gentleman told me that everything

worth knowing about me derives from the fact that I prefer meat to fish. I am by no means sure that I do, but I said that I would think about the matter. This sort of simplified anthropology being much in vogue, I have indeed thought it prudent to have answers ready, should the occasion arise again. I have compiled lists of things adequate to explain everything worth knowing about Japanese gentlemen. My chief trouble has been an inability to think of things unpleasant enough to offer some possibility of getting even. A fish market is by no means as unpleasant as a butcher shop.

The hot spring, which might well head the list, is very pleasant indeed. To describe it as the center of a peculiarly Japanese religious cult may seem extravagant; but there are all sorts of religions, and grand theories about the most basic impulses of a people have been built on flimsier foundations.

Edward G. Seidensticker

Shūgaku-ryokō
修学旅行
School excursions.

Along with the many forms of technological pollution that plague Japan like the rest of the world—industrial and traffic fumes, high levels of noise, and the mindless damage wrought upon nature—another form of annoyance troublesome to foreigners and locals alike tends to be overlooked in standard lists of public nuisances. I am referring to that special phenomenon labeled the "school excursion" and ostensibly aimed at exposing children to firsthand experience of the great natural, cultural, and artistic treasures of Japan.

The trouble usually begins right at the main gate of any temple, shrine, or building worthy of notice—if not already on the way there—with hapless passengers trapped in a railway car among droves of school lads and lassies doing their uproarious best to make themselves unbearable. After threading his way to the ticket window through a thick mass of jostling, sneering, and shrieking youngsters, and already tested to the limits of forbearance, the visitor walks into a temple compound like that of the ancient and beautiful Hōryū-ji in Nara, only to find himself in the thick of another crowd of black and navy-blue school uniforms, with horde upon horde of other small barbarians looming on the horizon.

As for the poor teachers trying to arouse some interest in their pupils for the wonders that surround them, they are quickly reduced to voices crying in the wilderness. Their charges are much too busy eyeing the foreigners and barking: *"Harō!"* ("Hello") at them to lend more than half an ear to explanations about some statue or building that has the fatal drawback of only being Japanese.

Way back when journeys were not everyday affairs, school excursions were part of the better educational curricula. They gave rural children some experience of the big cities, brought city children out to discover the treasures of the countryside, and provided solid nourishment for the youth who would one day be entrusted with carrying on the great traditions of Japan. The goal has not changed much through the years, but the children have. Blessed with far more opportunities for travel, whether alone or with family and friends, the once well-behaved schoolboys and schoolgirls of Japan have become like swarms of killer bees. And that makes a lot of people wonder if the purpose of such excursions might not in itself be in peril for the next generation of children.

By the middle of the afternoon, these endless uniformed processions begin to troop back to their buses and trains for the trip home. And throughout the land temples, castles, gardens, and museums would seem to heave a sigh of relief and relax once more into their former state of calm and civilization. Another school-excursion day is nearing its end, and the Buddhas, in their infinite forbearance, smile gently down on the remaining visitors.

Jacques Thiriet

Tebukuro, 手袋

Gloves.

I sometimes pity sociologists and other observers of Japan who go to such length to devise complicated techniques for measuring cultural change in this country, when there are much simpler and no less revealing barometers at hand in everyday things. One such gauge of how Japan is coping with modernity might seem to be a sign of successful modernization. Yet it is as typically Japanese as the *hachimaki* (headband), which you can see everywhere, and the *fundoshi* (loincloth), which you're usually not supposed to see. I refer to the wearing of gloves, especially white ones, and—alas—to their gradual abandonment in recent times.

One doesn't have to be very long in this country to appreciate how keen the Japanese are on formality and ceremony. Even if one has been here half a lifetime, it still comes as a culture shock to see a stationmaster in some God-forsaken country hamlet draw himself up to attention, square his shoulders, raise his white-gloved hand to his cap, and send you off with a salute no less dignified than that accorded the prime minister himself.

The use of white gloves is primarily, but not exclusively, the prerogative of railway employees and other public servants dedicated to keeping the country on the move: bus drivers, taxi chauffeurs, escalator operators, elevator attendants, and the like. However much you feel like a tinned sardine packed into the rush-hour public transportation system, a cursory glance at the spanking clean white gloves of the man who holds your fate in his hands is enough to sustain the illusion that you are enjoying the safety (if not the comfort) of a private limousine.

Since Japan started its rush toward democratization late in the nineteenth century, the culture of the high warrior class has been benignly extended to the populace as a whole. And as a result, the privilege of white-gloved service, symbolizing the shift to the new Western chic, could hardly be confined any longer to the rich and the powerful.

After the war it became customary for politicians on the campaign trail to wear white gloves when holding their microphones, but this practice is clearly on the wane. Could this, perhaps, reflect an impending decline in the high-quality service that, in Japan at least, has always been associated with white gloves?

Jan Swyngedouw

Seifuku, 制服

Uniforms.

There was something slightly sinister about it all at first: the students all in their dark uniforms with the same caps and black leather bags; the female bank employees all in the same colored skirts, white blouses, and jackets; the male white-collar workers each and every one sporting his dark suit, white shirt, tie, and gold company pin in the lapel. Never having accepted the cliché that all Japanese look alike, I found myself thinking that they surely have a tendency to dress alike, and that this must indicate some deep authoritarian frame of mind alien to us freedom-loving Americans.

Of course, those who spend most time talking about doing their "own thing" are the American university students with their nearly identical hair styles, the latest fashionable T-shirts, the same kind of blue jeans and track shoes. The difference seems to lie in the distinction between a uniform that one selects voluntarily and a uniform imposed on one by some organization or group. The mere appearance of uniformity does not tell the whole story.

Apparently no such distinction exists in Japan, where the range of customs and manners in which the group takes precedence over the individual is much broader than in the West. In Japan one must take into account a social background in which distinctions between voluntary and involuntary tend to get blurred, and where members of the "team" take pride in their membership, where their "uniform" is viewed as a reassuring symbol of group identity.

Approaching the matter from a purely aesthetic point of view, I would have to say that I find the traditional Japanese workmen's uniforms, some dating from the Edo period, when they were prescribed by law, quite attractive. There is the clean-looking, all-white dress of the sushi boys with their *hachimaki* (headband) and geta, and the carpenters and gardeners with their *haramaki* (belly-band), baggy breeches, and *jikatabi* (workman's footwear), and sometimes full body tattoos, a kind of permanent uniform.

The uniform, like the use of Western clothes in general, has become so much a part of Japan that the uneasiness of a people merely imitating foreign customs has all but entirely disappeared. However anachronistic Japanese business suits, boys' high-school uniforms, middle-school girls' sailor outfits, and the like may look to the Westerner newly arrived to the country, the Japanese themselves seem to regard these clothes with pride purely because of their deeper significance. The same sense, of course, belongs to traditional Japanese clothes. Even if they are reserved nowadays for special occasions, the national identity they carry is not to be overlooked. Many an enthusiastic foreigner donning *yukata* (cotton summer kimono) and geta at a Bon festival in some local village has felt the piercing stares of young Japanese in their domestically manufactured blue jeans, imitation Harvard sweatshirts, and track shoes, amazed at the foreigner who has the audacity to put himself inside one of *their* uniforms.

Joseph S. Lapenta

Surippa
スリッパ
House slippers.

Slippers came to Japan from the West, a fact that their indigenized name, *surippa,* is enough to give away. Possibly because of their shoes-off way of life, the Japanese have found themselves perfectly at home with the custom, so much so that Japan may be considered the most slipper-loving nation on earth.

In Japan slippers are more than mere footwear: they span the psychological space between the realms of shoes and of bare feet. As everyone knows, you take your shoes off when entering a Japanese home and are given a pair of soft, heelless slippers. These are worn for traversing the neutral or connecting spaces of the home: corridors, stairways, the kitchen. Only on the threshold of tatami-matted rooms do you leave your slippers behind. (Whether slippers are worn in carpeted rooms depends on the householder's preference.)

There is a definite etiquette connected with slippers. Toilets, for example, have their own slippers, usually made of slick plastic rather than the fabric of house slippers. The custom of having a different wardrobe for each season has also been extended to slippers, so that most people now put out different sets of house slippers for different seasons—warm woolly ones for winter, light cotton or straw for summer. A byproduct of this slipper syndrome, of course, is the plethora of attractive slippers of every conceivable design and color, leading one to suspect that the industry itself must be among the largest in the country. Department stores even stock "designer slippers" graced by the monograms of the likes of Yves St. Laurent and Pierre Cardin.

Switching from shoes to slippers to stocking feet and back may seem rather to complicate life. But once you get used to it, it becomes second nature. Indeed, you feel positively uncomfortable going unshod on slipper territory; and the reverse, of course, is almost as unthinkable as keeping your shoes on indoors. To give a concrete example: I live in a modest Japanese-style apartment with a kitchen area I can cross in three or four strides. Yet whenever I leave my tatami living room to pass through the kitchen to the bathroom on the other side, I automatically shuffle on my slippers. Just as automatically, I shed them at the toilet door and switch to the toilet slippers. Then, of course, the entire process is repeated on the return trip. And this may occur many times a day.

It has been observed that the Japanese compartmentalize their lives in order to retain psychological equilibrium in their congested environment. They create psychological space to compensate for the lack of physical space. The slipper phenomenon may be a minor manifestation of this survival mechanism. Certainly the demarcation, even in a tiny apartment, between slippered and unslippered territory gives the illusion of greater space by increasing the number of boundaries one has to cross.

Suzanne Trumbull

Jikatabi, 地下足袋

Workmen's rubber-soled, stockinglike footwear.

Workmen in Japan are most particular about their appearance. This is not to say that they are much concerned about what is going on in the fashion worlds of New York or Paris. It does, however, indicate their standard. This is *inase:* a snappy, clean-cut brand of machismo. Hair is cropped to a no-nonsense crew cut and the forehead is wrapped with a smart *hachimaki,* or calico band. A V-neck cotton shirt, immaculately clean, is usual nowadays, together with the traditional trousers that flair out at the thighs like riding breeches. And on the workman's feet comes his real pride—a good pair of *jikatabi.*

The string of Chinese characters with which the Japanese write the term gives the literal translation of jikatabi as "directly-on-the-earth foot-bags," which is not altogether a bad description. Soft and pliable, jikatabi preserve the sensitivity of the foot much in the manner of Indian moccasins. A split between the big toe and the others allows freedom of movement for bending and gripping. In effect, the feet are not shod but gloved.

Like tennis or basketball shoes, jikatabi are made of gabardine and soled with rubber. The best are dyed with indigo and have hand-sewn soles. They are fastened at the inside of the leg with metal tabs that form a closure neat as a zipper but more comfortable, and adjustable besides. Cleverly designed to hug the ankle and calf with nary a wrinkle, jikatabi support the muscles of the leg—and also show them off. All this combines to make them so indispensable to people who depend on their feet: gardeners perched on branches like tree frogs, carpenters picking their way along precarious beams, pilgrims treading rocky roads.

To be inase, the jikatabi must be tight and new. A foreman will often buy an expensive handmade pair, wear them a couple of times, and then pass them on to a subordinate, who is delighted to be standing in his boss's boots.

Jikatabi developed from *tabi,* the low, tight socks that are meant to be worn indoors or with zori. Plain tabi remain the usual

form of footwear for *mikoshi* palanquin bearers at shrine festivals. The ancestor of the modern-day jikatabi had a sole of thick cloth reinforced with heavy hand-stitched quilting. During World War II they comforted the feet of tank crewmen, for whom leather boots on the grilling steel floor would have been too hot.

The invention of rubber-soled tabi in 1923 helped to spread the popularity of the jikatabi all the way to China, providing manufacturers with an income far above that of the average artisan. One of the largest makers had the foresight to invest his profits in a technological extension of the foot—which is how Bridgestone, Japan's world-famous tire company, took its first step.

Patricia H. Massy

Yojōhan, 四畳半

A four-and-a-half mat room.

In recent decades the Japanese tea ceremony has gained an international reputation, and justifiably so. With the right combination of select tea utensils, skillful performers and knowledgeable guests, the ceremony is a rewarding exercise in beauty, grace, tranquillity, and subtlety. What adds to this atmosphere (or rather is an inseparable part of it) is the teahouse—not the large open room used so often these days to accommodate sizable groups, but the traditional *yojōhan* room.

Literally, yojōhan means "four and a half tatami mats." Although the size of tatami has varied to some extent according to period and region, the average size of a single mat has been about three by six feet, meaning that a yojōhan room measures approximately nine feet square. Of necessity, movement in such a narrow space is kept to a minimum. Every action must be economical and planned, all in harmony with the essence of the tea ceremony.

But there is more to the yojōhan than tea ceremonies. Resourceful people have adopted it for purposes less noble, though perhaps no less demanding. There is even a special word reserved for this "other" use: *yojōhan-shumi,* rendered somewhat pompously as "leisure activities in a four-and-a-half-mat room." The activities include drinking saké, singing traditional songs in subdued voice, and, most importantly, enjoying the companionship of a lady. This, the dictionaries tell us, is a most Japanese form of leisure activity, although it seems fair to state that there is something clearly universal at work here.

This latter connotation has brought the unpretentious little room into the limelight through a major legal battle over government censorship. The well-known novelist Nagai Kafū some time ago wrote a short story entitled "In the Four-and-a-Half-Mat Room," which describes the delights encountered in one such room in suggestive, often earthy, but never lascivious, language—at least not by present-day standards. It was not until 1972 that a Japanese literary magazine published the entire piece. The authorities promptly confiscated the issue and prohibited further publication, claiming that it was pornography, not literature. The case went to court and seven years later, after numerous appeals, the magazine was found guilty by the Japanese Supreme Court.

The yojōhan has another, more ordinary meaning for the average Japanese to whom lack of space is a familiar problem. Though today's apartments usually contain at least one such room, its inability to accommodate pianos, beds, and television sets threatens to make it soon a thing of the past. The trend nowadays is toward larger rooms of six or eight mats. And it seems fair to predict that in time, out of necessity, the tea ceremony and love tryst will follow suit and move to more spacious quarters.

Thomas J. Cogan

Okujō, 屋上

Rooftops.

The obvious choice for the visitor eager to observe life at a glance in some foreign land is the city park, but in a country like Japan with relatively few open spaces, public or private, the rooftop provides a convenient alternative. That's right—the rooftop. The *okujō*, the functional space atop most large buildings and many homes, is much more than a fire escape or sun deck; it is an extension of the building itself and offers a remarkably detailed microcosm of life as the urban Japanese live it.

If you have ever wondered in despair during the miserably hot summer why downtown Tokyo has virtually no sidewalk cafes, take the elevator up the nearest department store to the rooftop. There you will find the beer flowing and a good view of Japan: the kiddy rides, the bonsai exhibition, the gossiping housewives, the flirting couples, the chortling office workers. The scenery varies from rooftop to rooftop, but you will more often than not find a Shinto shrine displayed in one corner, amid a "natural" setting of potted trees and shrubs.

Department stores don't have a monopoly on okujō. Yardless houses in the more crowded residential neighborhoods, for example, commonly have balconylike structures built over the regular roofs to accommodate the washing or overflow storage. And most any office building has a variety of facilities that come to life during the brief noon recess—anything from wicker chairs to volleyball courts. Even the least appointed rooftop provides a spot for meditation, a cigarette, a confidental chat, or even (despite the perfunctory railings) a suicide—this leap down to the asphalt being one of the more popular methods.

Like the forested hills where Shinto shrines were originally erected, the okujō provides the urban dweller a place in which to enjoy relative solitude. Until building standards improved and "earthquake-proof" skyscrapers began appearing on the horizon about a decade ago, department stores used to be the tallest structures around. With few other buildings to obstruct the view, one

could, from atop a department-store okujō, succumb momentarily to the illusion of isolation. The sky is now more crowded; and as more and more skyscrapers congest the Tokyo skyline, I cannot help believing that the Japanese, entering an age in which shrines and parks and rooftops are no longer, will look for new ways to preserve that illusion of isolation. In the meantime, I for one shall continue using the top of some office building or department store for my lunch spot when I am brown-bagging it in Tokyo and a park bench is not near at hand. And I shall gaze down as ever on a city of mini-plazas on which, at street level, walkers will never set eyes.

Edward Fowler

Kagi, 鍵

Lock and key.

Kagi is not a subject I know much about. I live in a farming village, in an old Japanese house with wooden shutters and sliding doors, and like my neighbors have no way of locking my house. I have no use for keys and have never felt the need to visit a locksmith. At first I used to feel uneasy about that, but my neighbors assured me that burglars simply do not exist in the Japanese countryside. By experience I have come to understand how the same word, kagi, can be used for both "lock" and "key" in a society that does not depend on the distinction to protect its possessions.

Every foreigner living in Japan has his own examples of the legendary honesty of the people here. My own is leaving two bottles of wine on a crowded railway platform and finding them still there, hours later; my wife's is leaving her handbag in a Tokyo taxi and later being located by the driver, who was cruising the streets, at his own expense, looking for her.

Why are the Japanese so honest? Perhaps we should be asking why other peoples of the world are less so. One explanation is the uncommon closeness of Japanese groups, which makes individual dishonesty so rare (although organized crime is a major institution). Another is the great profusion of police stations: the tiny police boxes, or *kōban,* that you find on nearly every block. The modern Japanese policeman may be much more civil than his Edo-period predecessors, but he still does a lot of patrolling–indeed, enough to merit the name *omawari-san,* "Mr. Walk-around"–and doesn't miss much.

Another reason for the traditional honesty of the Japanese, it has been suggested, is that they usually have a *rusuban* (a friend or relative who stays at home to keep an eye on things) and often a *banken,* or watchdog, as well.

Getting back to the kagi. Basically keys in Japan are of two sorts, one made of bent wire, which was introduced from China more than a thousand years ago; and the familiar round European type, which was brought over by nineteenth-century traders from the West.

The modern Japanese living in city apartment blocks have learned the importance of locking their doors (though not so well that regular promotional campaigns sponsored by the police have become unnecessary); and the phenomenon of the "key children," who need to be able to let themselves in when they come home from school because their mothers are out working, shopping, or visiting friends, is a familiar one.

But you can still leave your wine on a railway platform or forget your purse in a taxi and hope to recover it later. Japan has yet to adopt *all* our light-fingered Western ways.

Murray Sayle

Mushi-kago
虫籠
Insect cages.

"A land of insects!" That was how I first came to look on Japan. Never in all my life had I seen such large grasshoppers. Compared with them, those I had left behind in England were mere ants. Some of the mosquitoes were large enough, and their bites were even larger. I won't speak about the fleas. But let me dwell a moment on another insect, one that we do not have in England except in books.

It was late summer when I arrived in Japan. I had expected to hear the song of Japanese birds; but alas, they were all silent. Even had they tried to sing, they would have been silenced by the noise—I can hardly call it "song"—of the cicada. And what a noise it is! Quite deafening, yet curiously fascinating. Never have I heard a drowsier sound than that of the cicada among Japanese pine trees on a hot summer afternoon. No wonder there are so few birds to be heard in summertime. They are all but silenced by the cicada.

Not long after my arrival I was surprised again by the odd behavior of some Japanese children. They had boxes or jars in one hand, and with the other they were trying to catch some invisible creature. Then I heard the sound of the cicada and I realized what they were after. Then, too, I caught my first glimpse of one, held between the thumb and forefinger of a boy. He held it with a mixture of tenderness and unconcern, before putting it in his box with the rest of his crawling collection.

Here is something I have often noticed about the Japanese in general. We English have a reputation of being fond of animals, yet we rarely pay much attention to insects, except perhaps ladybirds and butterflies. The Japanese, on the other hand, seem to have a special affinity with insects. Whether they love the insects for their sound, or loathe them for their smell, they are seldom indifferent to them. As for the cicada and other singing insects, it isn't only the children who pursue them and prize them; Japanese of all ages like to keep them in bamboo cages and enjoy their soothing song in late summer and early autumn.

Once I had the idea of getting my students to write "mini-essays" for me about insects. Some wrote about ants, others about bees, others about centipedes, and yet others about cockroaches—though toward these latter they had no friendly feeling. In all the essays, whether friendly or otherwise, I was impressed by the students' perceptive as well as imaginative response. They all knew what they were talking about, and they infused a feeling into their knowledge, such as one rarely finds among Westerners. In this, it seemed to me, they came close to Coleridge's ideal of loving "all things both great and small."

Peter Milward

Kō, 香

Incense.

When Buddhism came into Japan in the sixth century, incense was one of the things that came with it. Aromatic woods—aloe, for instance—pulverized and mixed with other aromatic substances and adhesives, then formed into pastes or sticks, were burned as purification and offering in Buddhist temples. Ambergris and the civet being probably unknown to the Japanese of earlier times, incense made the wealthy and elegant fragrant. Noblemen and their ladies burned incense in special containers under their clothes before donning them to ensure that they were accompanied by a pleasing ambience as they went their refined and ceremonious ways.

As time passed, incense became more than religious purification or frivolous fragrance. In the Heian period, aristocrats loved games in which things were matched. They played the poem-matching game, the shell-matching game, and a game in which fragrances of incense were matched. In the late fifteenth and early sixteenth centuries, incense matching was converted into a ritualized, artistic pursuit combining extensive knowledge of aromatic woods and great familiarity with classical literature, which was incorporated in the incense games. This evolved into what is known as *Kōdō,* or the Way of Incense, the devotees of which insist that the incense ceremony, its atmosphere, and its cultural associations have ethical as well as entertainment value.

The Way of Incense has always entailed expensive luxury. Apparently a pastime like this one, which demands financial outlay, leisure, and literary knowledge, would find little favor in busy modern Japan. And, to be sure, it is not the favorite activity of most men in the street. Nonetheless it is still alive, as the occasional television commercial for incense implements suggests.

On a lowly, but essential plane, the Japanese employ something else that goes by the name of incense: *katorisenkō* (a word that might be translated as "incense to take care of the mosquitoes"). To make it, the flowers and leaves of a certain kind of chrysanthemum, containing a substance that attacks insect nervous and muscular systems but is harmless to man, are dried, mixed with dyes (usually green) and adhesives, and pressed into coils, which are lighted on summer nights to keep away pesky insects.

Containers for katorisenkō range from purely functional to fanciful. Miniature ceramic or iron house-shaped burners have removable roofs permitting the installation of the slow-burning coil. More amusing are the ceramic hippopotamuses and pigs in which the coils are suspended and through whose gaping mouths the mosquito-slaying smoke curls. Modern technology has not left katorisenkō untouched. Today many people prefer to use little electric heaters with impregnated pads that, when warmed, fill the night air with an artificially sweetish scent that, while dealing bugs the quietus, lacks the charm of the smoke wending its way out of houses and hippopotamuses.

Richard L. Gage

Kigumi, 木組

Wood joinery.

After touring a shrine, a temple, or an imposing old farmhouse, it is easy to appreciate the fact that Japan enjoys the most highly developed wood-construction techniques in the world. An essential part of this craft is *kigumi,* or wood joinery, with its several hundred different joints. Kigumi has managed to survive modernization and the increasing use of metal and concrete because it is more than just a carpenter's art. In one form or another, kigumi is found almost everywhere one looks in Japan—from the old-fashioned *masu,* or wooden measuring cups, now used for saké to the most splendidly crafted furniture.

No doubt Japan's earliest builders turned to wood centuries ago for the simple reason that trees were so abundant in Japan—as stone and clay have never been. But wooden structures have been preferred here for other reasons, too. One is a direct benefit of kigumi: the many joints required in wooden structures act as shock absorbers during an earthquake. A well-constructed wooden building may shake a great deal during a tremor, even enough to leave the structure out of true; but if it survives the first shock, it will rarely collapse. I am told that until not so many years ago it was not uncommon to see wooden buildings being winched back into true after an earthquake—clearly an option not offered by concrete construction.

Physically and aesthetically, wood is much nicer than concrete to live with. And being a natural material, wood responds to nature. Wood does not sweat or get clammy when the weather is humid (although when dresser drawers or sliding partitions stick during the rainy season, one is reminded that wood does absorb moisture and swell), and it is never unpleasant to the touch, even in the bitterest cold of winter. But perhaps the most important reason that wood continues to have appeal as a structural material is that it is a living thing and therefore endowed with spirit. From ancient times the Japanese have believed in the inherent spirit of a tree: a spirit that does not disappear even when the tree is turned

into lumber. Hence it is not only the skill of the craftsman but also the very life of the wood itself that attracts one in a beautifully worked, satiny pillar, in a glowing, polished staircase, or in a magnificent old chest. And it may be a respect for the spirit that resides in the wood that accounts for both the usual Japanese reluctance to paint worked wood, whether a structure or a piece of furniture, and the practice of scouring or planing old wood to renew both its freshness and its scent.

Each day ferroconcrete structures become more numerous. But somehow, looking at my own largely wood apartment constructed in a concrete shell, I cannot help thinking that as long as there are people in Japan to appreciate the life and inner beauty of wood, we will always find kigumi around us.

Rebecca M. Davis

Washi, 和紙

Japanese paper.

When I first came to Japan I was impressed by the elaborate way in which everything purchased was wrapped in paper. The packages were invariably neat and often artistic. Even at the fish market or vegetable stall it seemed impossible to sell anything without the inevitable scrap of old newspaper to wrap it in. To give it "naked" was considered rude. But what most fascinated me were the sheets of beautiful Japanese paper, or *washi*—each one unique, each a work of art.

Paper was first produced in China about A.D. 100 and brought to Japan about the year 600. Prince Shōtoku himself is said to have encouraged its production by ordering the planting of hemp and paper-mulberry trees. At first used for religious, and later for governmental, documents, the art of paper making spread to the provinces and became a winter trade for many farmers.

Whereas in the West papyrus and parchment were expensive and used mainly by the aristocracy, in Japan paper quickly became a popular material used by nearly every class of society. As early as the fourteenth century popular storybooks printed from wood blocks on washi were available to the common people, greatly increasing the literacy rate. Sketch books from the same period also attest to the use of scraps left over from writing for toilet paper and postpartum cleansing—which may well be the first case of recycling in history.

Although paper was introduced in connection with Buddhism, it is Shinto that has given paper its special significance and religious associations. (In Japanese, *kami* can mean either a Shinto god or paper.) To this day, pure white washi is attached to the *shimenawa* (a ceremonial rope marking off a patch of holy ground), and is an integral part of many Shinto ceremonies.

Washi is hand made, often in mountain villages where there is a plentiful supply of pure water. Traditional methods are still used. Fibers are cleaned, soaked, boiled, pounded, and mixed in a thick emulsion. Thin sheets of the tangled fibers are removed, dried on boards in the sun, and then peeled off to become paper of amazing strength, versatility, and beauty.

Since the Meiji era, mass-produced Western-style paper has replaced washi in most areas of modern life, but washi has survived and is still highly valued by the Japanese. It is used in sliding doors, in paper windows, in lanterns, in folding screens, and for the art of origami, where its flexibility makes it especially well suited. Much of Japan's art, calligraphy, and bookmaking would be impossible without it. And even the bit of charm that it gives umbrellas, fans, kites, and a host of other things in Japanese daily life reminds us of this important facet of Japan's cultural heritage.

Beverley D. Tucker

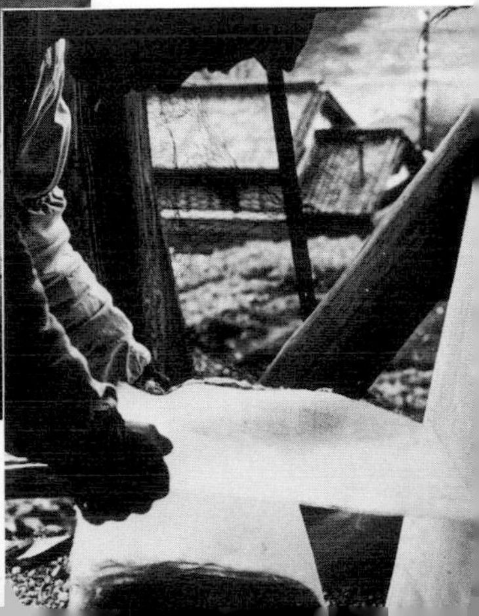

Noshi, のし

Gift decorations.

Although occasions for gift giving in Japan have changed with the times, certain old customs have survived. Formerly, for instance, fish and wine were traditional gifts for celebrations and consolation. Such gifts were wrapped in beautiful paper and colored strings, the final knot being tied to resemble the silkworm butterfly, symbol of health and fertility. The practice continues today in a piece of special paper on which the donor's dedication is inscribed and which is bound with a pair of knotted cords, or *mizuhiki.* The colors used for these paper cords, of which there may be five, seven, or nine, depend on the occasion. Gold and silver are customary for weddings; white and crimson for general greetings; white and black or light gray for funerals. To the upper right and above the strings is affixed (or nowadays, printed) the symbolic, fishlike little *noshi.*

The noshi was originally a thin strip of dried *awabi,* or ear-shell, that had been stretched to indicate long life and protection from harm (the awabi does not decompose), and was neatly folded in a small paper gusset. Since the Muromachi period, this ensemble represented the awabi offered for refreshment to the household of the shogun at the famous Ōgusaya Inn in Ise when they came to worship at the imperial shrine.

One of the most remarkable customs of Japan is the sizable amounts of cash given as presents for everything from weddings to the matriculation into university of a niece or nephew, to the *otoshidama* money given to children at New Year's, to tips to the staff of one's favorite restaurant. If someone close passes away, cash may be given to the family of the deceased as a *kōden* (money given in place of incense, to help defray burial expenses). In each case, though, cash is never presented "naked," but is enclosed in a proper packet; in celebration, the packet is topped with a noshi and called a *noshibukuro.* This custom of not giving money without wrapping it up beautifully stems in part from the Japanese way of thinking of money as something vulgar. But it

should also be seen in light of the fact that Japanese do not like to show their minds too openly, and hence do not as a rule open gifts in the presence of the giver. Even if the recipient knows the contents of the packet, opening it might excite jealousy in one of the parties, which would cause bad feelings all around. In this sense, one might call the noshibukuro a sort of general cultural defense mechanism.

Jean Esmein

Nihontō, 日本刀

The Japanese sword.

Like the cherry blossom, which a famous eighteenth-century poem of Moto-ori Norinaga immortalized as the very reflection of the heart of Japan, the sword represents another of its great spiritual symbols. For besides being the very "soul of the warrior" and a formidable weapon in the hands of a master, it is also and above all else a highly beautiful work of art, epitomizing one of the main aesthetic ideas of Japanese craftsmen and artists: the search for soul through purity and simplicity in formal beauty. It is pure spirit molded in steel.

That the Japanese sword is infinitely much more than a weapon is obvious to anyone who has watched a man fortunate enough to own one in the act–or rather in the ceremony–of polishing his treasure as a means of enjoying a quiet evening of mind-relaxing pleasure.

Look at him, seated in proper fashion in an atmosphere of perfect silence. First he unwraps the sword from its silken bag and then seizes the scabbard in his left hand in a quiet, deliberate gesture, pulling out the blade with an unhesitating yet slow and reverential movement of the right hand. Watch him hold the sword up to the light and gaze at the elegance of the blade's curvature, slowly, ever so slowly, from the hilt to the point, all the while admiring the gently undulating patterns of the tempered line. Then he removes the old oil from the blade with a small red bag containing finely powdered stone. After two wipings with thick Japanese paper, the blade stands in its full gleaming glory, and seems to justify the view commonly held among knowledgeable critics that for workmanship, quality, and sheer naked beauty, the Japanese sword far surpasses anything ever produced in Toledo or Damascus ("mere kitchen cutlery when compared to the Japanese sword," in the words of a famous nineteenth-century Italian swordsmith).

It is no wonder then that this most perfect steel sword has always been the object of a respect bordering on worship. Along

Appraisal by Hon'ami Nisshū.

with the Mirror and the Beads, the so-called Grass-Cutting Sword has been, since the dawn of Japanese history, one of the three regalia ensuring the authority of the emperor; and its spiritual value is so highly regarded that the noted Edo-period monk Takuan wrote a treatise on the philosophy of Zen Buddhism with similes entirely based on the sword.

Some Japanese scholars have even attempted to give a curious psychological basis to the ritual suicide by disembowlment: the warrior's death by his own weapon is the ultimate act of worship toward the impossible beauty of the Japanese sword. One may dismiss the theory as too farfetched, or claim that it applies only to the short sword used for hara-kiri (or more correctly, *seppuku*). But anyone who has once held and admired a *nihontō* may feel that there is perhaps some truth in it after all.

Jean-René Cholley

Sensu
扇子
The folding fan.

The oil-producing countries keep hiking the price of oil and the rest of the world is busy trying to dream up new ways to conserve energy. In Japan, the *uchiwa,* or round, one-piece fan, and the *sensu,* or folding fan, are experiencing a revival, with supplies barely able to keep pace with demand. What better way to make a quick bit of breeze and offer oneself or another a moment's respite from the summer's heat! And with its bamboo slats and strong *washi* (Japanese paper), the sensu can be folded and unfolded with the greatest of ease.

Revered in China as one of the "Eight Precious Things" of Taoist symbolism, the fan is surrounded with legends that put its origins as far back as the second or third milennium B.C. Yet it is a Japanese who is credited with inventing the folding fan as we know it today—in imitation, it is said, of the wing of a bat.

Aside from occasional periods of popularity, the fan has not been widely used in the West, tending to be associated more with royalty than with the common man. In China and Japan, on the other hand, it underwent a development of another scale altogether. By the middle ages it was a common accessory for all classes of people, and thence found its way into ceremonial and artistic uses as well. Like the folding screen, it attracted the skills of many a famous artist and calligrapher.

Among the variety of reasons for Japan's surviving attachment to the fan are her fondness for delicate utensils, her love of washi, and the irreplaceable effect of having a picture suddenly appear at the flick of a wrist. The fan has other associations as well. Its pivot, or *kaname,* from which the face is opened up and folded back into hiding again, has become a synonym for the "core" or "nucleus" of a thing. Similarly, the manner in which the fan spreads out from a single point to a wide area is called *suehiro* and becomes a natural idiom for good fortune and prosperity in the future. The appearance of the fan in a great number of ceremonies in Japan depends on this symbolic meaning.

In the hands of a skilled dancer or Kabuki actor, the fan can be made to simulate a wide range of visual and emotional effects: winds and waves, birds and flowers, swords and goblets, the violent disturbances of the heart, pain and joy. In much the same way, the traditional Japanese comic storyteller uses only a single sensu to create the environment of actions and sounds that accompany his dialogue.

Along with the reopening of the country during the Meiji era, the trend toward things American since World War II, and the remarkable drive for technological innovation we find at present, Japan's experiment with modernization has seemed to go hand in hand with a growing disregard for what is uniquely its own. Thus, the sensu gives way to the electric fan and the air conditioner, leaving the white wedding fan and the distinctive fan of traditional dance behind as relics. But the roots of tradition reach much deeper than the forces of modernization, and it takes only the right set of circumstances for Japan's unshaken trust in the past to revive. The fact that the energy crisis has brought the fan back into everyday use is one such indication of the survival of the past in contemporary Japan.

Karl Manougian

Hanga, 版画

A print; a woodblock print.

Kamiyui, by Mori Yoshitoshi.

There are still some who think of the Japanese print in terms of *ukiyoe,* those fascinating and exotic masterworks of the past, printed in water color with hand-cut cherry-wood blocks. In fact, the word *hanga,* or print, now has much broader associations. Its materials range from wood to cloth to copper and other metals. What is more, the contemporary Japanese artist is so active on the world art scene, and so modern in his approach, that neither style nor subject matter can be said to reflect nationality as they once did in the ukiyoe prints.

One of the universally popular print-making techniques of Japan involves the use of a fine mesh to secure parts of a stencil. It is a technique that, in fact, owes its origins to the indigenous stencil used three hundred years ago as a textile-printing device. Later changes in technique and materials served to simplify the process. Still, there are artists who continue to use the ancient textile-stencil method to produce their prints. Among them are Mori Yoshitoshi and Kawada Kan, both of whom share a devotion to truly Japanese subjects as well. Given the impossibility of describing the diversity of forms that hanga take in contemporary Japan, a glance at these two artists, and their attempts to weld the best of the traditional to the best of the modern, should prove enlightening.

In the art of Mori Yoshitoshi an exceptional visual memory comes together with the direct experience of life in Japan before modernization to produce a reliable document of the turn of the century. Although he was born in 1898, the passing years have in no way lessened the vitality and dynamic effect of each new stencil print. Busy craftsmen, joyous dancers, temple performers of the folksy life of his generation all seem to burst with energy. Whether recording the fierceness of an ancient battle scene or the almost abstract curves of a courtly love scene, Mori's visual expression conveys the story in a way that is unmatched. *Kamiyui,* the professional hairdresser of the past, is one of his craftsman series and shows strand upon strand being pulled, tied, padded, and distorted into those fashionable hairdos we see in old illustrations. Mori's sly sense of humor conveys something of the torture the customer endured.

Kanazawa in the Snow is typical of Kawada Kan's preference for the unique patterns common to ancient Japanese architecture —the checked design of paper-covered doors, the stripes found in wooden grids, the effects of parallel lines seen in perspective in bamboo fences and tiled roofs. Kawada delights in recording the wooden carpentry of exposed interior beams, the accent of edged floor mats, and all those abstract design qualities that add up to pleasing compositions. Through his stencil prints, Kawada is preserving for posterity the structural beauty of these fast disappearing scenes of the old Japan.

Frances Blakemore

Kanazawa in the Snow, by Kawada Kan.

Imari, 伊万里

A type of ceramic pottery.

"Paintings are for looking at, but ceramics are meant to be touched." The collector's eyes seemed to caress the vase as I turned it gingerly in my hands. "The pleasurable weight and heavy creaminess of the porcelain with the blue underglaze grasses defined in a few vivid brushstrokes," he went on, "mark it clearly as early Imari."

The story of pottery in Japan reaches back into prehistory, some ten thousand years ago, but as an art form it was influenced heavily by the mainland and brought to one reform after another. An interesting part of this story concerns what can be called the "pottery war," which took place during the war between Japan and Korea in the sixteenth century, when Japan's military generals tried to outdo one another in capture and in bringing back to the homeland Korea's best potters, to develop the art of ceramics. One of the main centers of this activity in Japan was the district of Arita in northern Kyushu, from which the whole range of carefully colored and intricately decorated wares known as Arita ware derives. Those artifacts were then exported in great quantities to European markets from the port of Imari (not only to adorn the living rooms of the upper classes, but in time to inspire and influence all the famous currents of European pottery as well). Hence the common name, Imari.

The use of overglaze techniques in the multicolored wares of Imari permit surface scenes of exquisite detail that the West has found captivating. But for me it is the dance of the *sometsuke* (blue-and-white dyeing) brush on simple water jars, vases, bowls, *soba* (buckwheat noodles) cups, and deep round dishes that I find most enchanting. Early Imari seems to awaken the sense of touch and transport one into contact with the clay itself. Then, too, it calls to mind what must have been a heart-rending search for those first Korean artists until they succeeded in discovering, in a foreign land, a white clay suitable for porcelain fire that would enable them to develop the art of ceramics they had left behind.

"Of course," the collector concluded his story, "after Sen no Rikyū introduced the rustic aesthetic into the tea ceremony in the sixteenth century, the less-perfect Korean ware made for daily use became very popular. The later Imari ware lost its roughness and became quite perfect. But earlier pieces, like this one, are identical to porcelains produced in Korea."

I was astonished. I had indeed seen wonderful porcelains in Korea, both ancient and modern, and I understood the beauty of their imperfections and the feel of the potter's hands. But the piece in my hands *was,* as far as I could tell, perfectly shaped on all sides. If this had been produced by the same school of Korean potters, I could only conclude that something momentous had happened to their sensibilities in the course of that fateful journey from Korea to Japan.

Sharon Ann Rhoads

Urushi, 漆

Lacquer ware.

The small city of Wajima in Ishikawa Prefecture is one of several places in Japan famous for lacquerware. Walking through its shops one can still sense the eighteenth century, when lacquering first became a commercial enterprise there. "Ah! This is the real thing," murmurs a visitor to one of the shops. The "real thing" is a dish, a tray, a box, or a pair of chopsticks having that unique finish that can come only from the application of at least twenty, and often more, film-thin layers of a mixture of sap from the lacquer tree and oil to a wooden base. Each layer takes a good deal of time to dry, but the final result is a light but sturdy, hard, and glossy smooth surface.

The art of lacquering is peculiar to Asia, having developed in response to the climate, vegetation, and cultural tastes of the countries where it is practiced. The unexcelled height of craftsmanship that it reached in Japan is acknowledged by the fact that the verb "to japan" has become accepted jargon for "to lacquer." Although originally imported from China, the art of *urushi* spread widely in Japan and developed into a variety of local styles, from thick, almost rough pieces to thin, shell-like vessels of great delicacy.

The main qualities of urushi are its beauty and its durability. In eighth- to tenth-century Japan, the basic black or red ground was augmented with color to beautify tableware, the *fubako* (letter boxes) of nobles, tools, and religious implements; and in the fourteenth century lacquer was used to adorn weaponry as well. Throughout the long peace of the Edo period artisans produced lovely lacquered tables, *jūbako* (tiered boxes), chests, bowls, and the like, which they inlaid with mother-of-pearl, garnished with gold leaf, or decorated with engraved designs. These designs ranged from intricate multicolored scenes, nature motifs, and mythological creatures to poetry and prose inscriptions.

It was perhaps only after the Meiji era that lacquered wares became more widely available to the common people. But today's rising costs have once again made the "real thing" too expensive for everyday use. Even a simple soup bowl will run at least $20, and more elaborate ones sell for many times that price. Still, in spite of the sacrifice it means for the family budget, people continue to purchase urushi wares as gifts for special occasions, for ceremonial use, or as tableware for guests. Since Japanese cooking is a "visual cuisine," urushi is still held to be indispensable for the maximum effect, and is also well suited to holding the most tongue-scalding of soups. (Lacquered ware does not crack with such use in Japan, as it would in the drier climates of Europe.)

Nowadays, cheap plastic imitations abound. To the undiscerning eye they may be impossible to distinguish from the "real thing," but the feel, color, and luster of even the best imitations cannot compare. As long as Japan's deep attachment to and respect for the small family workshop and traditional handicrafts remain, there is hope that this art will survive well into the future.

Patricia Murray

Teien, 庭園

Landscape gardens.

The Japanese garden, it is said, is a kind of earth sculpture that begins with a respect for the original surface of the ground. The basic materials are not man-made but natural, and the arrangement of hills, ponds, trees, and rocks is made to trace the path of nature itself. In the rock garden of Kyoto's famous temple Ryōan-ji, the fine white gravel represents the waters of the sea and the larger rocks the small islands that float on its surface. At the same time, the round and elliptical clusters of rocks are considered to be sacred space for enshrining the gods. For the rock, as a kind of concentrated form of infinite space, shares the kind of fullness of existence associated with the gods. This very abstruseness is the quintessence of the garden's beauty.

In the midst of Ryōan-ji's rock garden, or surrounded by the panorama of Kyoto's imperial villa Katsura Rikyū, one comes to sense the way in which the Japanese garden's use of space both draws one into the scene and yet keeps one at a distance. Its nearly perfect composition tends to take away one's breath, and yet insight into its spiritual beauty and its principles of composition is taken to be a way of purifying the soul. What enjoyment there is in the Japanese garden is not one of superficial relaxation.

During the baroque period in Europe gardens were numerous, both those that were kept in a "natural" and untamed state and those of highly manicured beauty. In both types, the bowers, the preserves for birds and fish, the classical statues enveloped in a ring of linden trees, the long rows of poplars, the walls of hedge and flowers, the benches, and the like, serve to remind us that in addition to the often remarkable harmony between architecture and nature, the gardens were put to some practical use as well. In such a garden one could relax in natural surroundings.

In the Japanese garden the echo of a waterfall or the trickle of a tiny stream is more like the resonance of a tower bell in a great stone cathedral for the sense of peace it brings to the soul. The strength of the garden's composition is such that it can never be

perfectly natural, not even in its achievement of sacred space. Bird droppings on the rock garden of Ryōan-ji or moles crawling in and out of the carefully shaped and trimmed shrubbery of Katsura Rikyū would be like ink spilled on a *sumi-e* painting. The intimacy that once existed between the garden and those of a bygone era who made it is denied us who did not share in its creation nor find in it a sense of common existence. Rather it is the nostalgia for the beauty of another world of eternally irretrievable illusions that the garden preserves for us and that we must preserve in the garden.

Čiháková Vlasta

Shakuhachi, 尺八

A vertical bamboo flute.

Bamboo and wind, as much a part of Japan as the rising sun, are brought together in the haunting, plaintive music of the *shakuhachi.* Its purity is the purity of all flutes: the human breath, closest to the inner soul, passing through a simple reed and becoming sound, the sound of life itself. But its history is a complex blend of the profane and the sacred.

Although its roots may reach as far back as ancient Egypt, the shakuhachi came to Japan from China. The Chinese five-holed

Shakuhachi, played by Yamaguchi Gorō.

flute, which used a Chinese pentatonic scale, was brought to Japan during the eighth century for use in the *Gagaku* court music. It was called shakuhachi simply because it measured one *shaku* and eight (*hachi*) *sun* in length (54.5 cm.).

In the fifteenth century a bamboo flute somewhat shorter than the shakuhachi was adopted by religious mendicants, but it was not until the Edo period that the shakuhachi as we know it today appeared. A sect of Zen priests made up of masterless samurai, or *komusō,* formed an alliance in Kyoto known as the Fukeshū. With a temple as their headquarters, they traveled from door to door and from village to village, faces hidden under large, basketlike hats, playing their shakuhachi. Some would have it that they served as spies for the shogun's government. Be that as it may, the religious significance of these wandering musicians lay not in the simple enjoyment of music but in a focusing of the spirit to overcome the passions of the flesh–hence the suggestion of otherworldly mystery in the tones of the shakuhachi.

During the Edo period the light, narrow bamboo flute was redesigned by the komusō, who made their instruments from the heavy, root end of the plant. In time of peril, this longer flute was used as a stout club.

Out of this rather unusual history comes today's gracefully curved bamboo flute, with its meticulously manicured and lacquered bore. The sound is made by blowing onto the outer edge of the mouthpiece, much as one might blow into a glass bottle. The five holes produce the near-pentatonic D, F, G, A, and C. Fingering techniques plus the raising and dropping of the jaw permit a range of additional notes in between. The achievement of proper tone and vibrato takes at least three years; their refinement is the essential element in mastery of the shakuhachi. The melody is subtly fragmented, with some of its tones nearly inaudible, creating an impression of gentle melancholy.

While the shakuhachi is not a musical instrument for parties or sing-alongs, in modern times it has been used in accompaniment with such diverse instruments as the samisen and the piano. Still, its dominant images of solitude, quiet, and introspection remain. It is the sound of wind and bamboo.

Wayne Murphy

Taiko, 太鼓

The Japanese drum.

What associations does the sound of a *taiko,* or drum, bring to mind? No doubt there are many and these will vary from individual to individual because the taiko turns up in so many of the arts and popular celebrations of Japan. But chances are that most Japanese, and most foreigners who have lived in Japan for any length of time, will immediately tend to associate the beat of the taiko with the joyful atmosphere of a festival. Many a Japanese can count among the earliest and happiest recollections of childhood the unmistakable roll of the drum filling the air on festival days.

A festival without drums would be unthinkable in Japan. Together with the flute and bells that also figure commonly in *bakabayashi* (festival music), the drums provide just the right background for the traditional celebration: primitive yet sophisticated rhythms, spontaneous and carefree noise with the proper touch of solemnity. One of the particular charms of the bakabayashi is its unassuming character: it sets the tone without becoming the focus of attention. Indeed drummers are sometimes hidden completely from view, riding on the inside of festival floats. This self-effacing quality of the festival musicians serves, for example, to direct the attention of the crowds to the most important element of a Shinto festival, the procession of portable shrines.

The drum patterns for festival music are repetitive and deceptively simple. I never realized just how complicated they were until I began learning how to play the taiko some twelve years ago. The first thing that surprises one is the lack of musical notation and the reliance on rhythmic syllable patterns, which the drummer fixes firmly in his memory before ever picking up the drumsticks. Each performer memorizes the pattern for the entire ensemble so that it is possible for the musicians to rotate on any of the several regular-sized drums or the large bass drum (*ōdaiko*). Once these patterns have been absorbed, it is difficult to erase them from one's brain. Although I have not touched a taiko in several years now, I find the mnemonic syllables (ten-te-ka ten-te-ka to-to ten-ten) for some patterns still come back to mind rather easily.

In recent years the taiko has been rediscovered in Japan. Professional drum groups specializing in traditional taiko performances are much in demand for wedding receptions, university festivals, and all kinds of celebrations. Each year the National Theater presents programs of various sorts of traditional drum music gathered from all over Japan. The prominent contemporary composer Ishii Maki has written a brilliant piece for the Ondeko-za drum ensemble and full orchestra, and is planning a European tour with them.

All of this is quite as it should be, for the taiko deserves to be recognized for the exciting sounds that the skilled performer can draw out of it. Yet somehow I still prefer to hear it outside of the concert hall, far from the hushed atmosphere of the National Theater, close to its simple origins in a rural shrine or echoing through Tokyo's old districts at festival time.

William Currie

Taiko, played by Ondeko-za.

Kanze Yoshiyuki in the Nō drama *Taihei Shōjō.*

Nō, 能

Nō drama.

Nō drama often seems to be a theater of memories and dreams. The beauty of a famous courtesan wilts with age and eventually the woman herself is taken by death. Only then, as a ghost, does she become the subject of a Nō play and tell of her memories of life. A medieval general wins countless battles and changes the course of Japanese history, but he too finds his role in Nō only when he returns from the dead and appears in the dream of a wandering priest.

The Nō is also a theater of strict form and convention. A

mother finds her infant son dead, yet raises no wail; she merely lifts both arms and brings her outstretched hands before her eyes in the strongest expression of grief the conventions of Nō allow. A traveler going to sleep does not lie down on stage, but simply raises his open fan with his left hand and hides his face.

Neither the memories and dreams, nor the strict form and convention were part of the Nō at its birth, however. The art from which Nō originally developed was closer to what we might think of as a circus. In the fourteenth and fifteenth centuries, several men—the most outstanding of whom was Zeami (1363–1443)—transformed the Nō and gave it those characteristics that make it so distinctive today.

Any given Nō play is put together from a large, but limited group of interchangeable parts. The text is written into a framework of traditional song forms. The instrumental music, played on three drums and a shrill bamboo flute, is strung together in fixed melodic and rhythmic patterns. The dance, which often forms the visual climax of a Nō play, is composed of a sequence of regulated patterns of movement. The mask, which becomes the focal point of the central character's dramatic expressiveness, is also chosen from a defined group of masks. Even the way the actors walk is strictly determined. Virtually all aspects of a Nō play, except the words of the text itself, are derived from some preexisting group of interchangeable parts. A play is held together and given unity by what we might call a theme, rather than a plot. Sometimes it is a Shinto miracle, sometimes a scene from an old legend, sometimes it is a poem. The theme may make its entrance into the play in what seems to be an almost accidental manner, but gradually as it recurs, various images and emotions become associated with it. The gradual accretion of image and emotion creates depth.

In an age of dramatic naturalism, one might expect the Nō to be an anachronism, an heirloom preserved not for its inherent beauty but for its "historical significance." Steadily increasing audiences and the growing interest shown by poets, actors, and students from all over the world prove this is not the case. For the dreams and memories of Nō capture our imaginations.

Thomas W. Hare

Kyōgen, 狂言

Comic theatrical skits.

Kyōgen is the oldest indigenous form of Japanese classical theater and as such has exerted a strong influence on all subsequent styles of theater in Japan. The entire art finds its roots in the *Sanbasō* fertility dance that is a major part of the Nō play *Okina*. In each of its 257 independent comic plays, Kyōgen celebrates the same vigorous life force that is expressed in ceremonial form in this Sanbasō dance. And while the characters that appear are feudal lords, servants, farmers, priests, and merchants who lived in Japan more than six hundred years ago, the situations in which they are presented and the manner in which they react to each other are no different from our lives today—they try to outwit each other, they quarrel and make up, and their lives seem to go on in a general atmosphere of optimistic good humor. Thus it is also the most universally relevant of Japan's traditional theater forms.

Kyōgen deals with the subplot of everyday human relations. It reveals the way our natural, untrammeled selves would really prefer to react to everyday situations—the stream-of-consciousness fantasies that rage through our brains as we face the little unpleasantries demanded of us by sophisticated society—the world of the daydream. But just as in real life, bothersome reality never ceases to intrude into those daydreams.

Kyōgen staging is simple in the extreme. The average number of characters is only two or three. There are no sets or special lighting. Masks are seldom used, and there is no makeup. The costumes are in subdued colors and only serve to indicate the social position of the character. Also, very few properties are used—most things are mimed using only a single folding fan, which every character carries tucked into his sash on the left side when not in use. Even facial expression is kept to a minimum, so that dramatic expression is achieved almost exclusively through the stylized vocal and physical forms and the spatial relationships among the performers on the stage. Thus the entire art of Kyōgen is completely de-

Nomura Manzō and Nomura Mannojō in the Kyōgen play *Hagi Daimyō*.

pendent for its dramatic effect upon the concentration and skill of the actor.

Kyōgen has, for these reasons, kept me so fascinated for the twenty years since I first came to Japan that I began taking lessons from the internationally famous actor Nomura Mansaku fifteen years ago and formed my own troupe five years ago for the purpose of presenting Kyōgen in English. The dialogue, for the most part, works very easily into English; and the universal humanity of content makes it easy for anyone to understand, since it deals with basic everyday situations.

Don Kenny

Bunraku, 文楽

Traditional puppet theater.

Puppets manipulated by Yoshida Tamao and Yoshida Minosuke in the Bunraku play *Sonezaki Shinjū.*

At the age of eleven, I was taken to my first *Bunraku* performance by Sugimoto Etsu, author of *A Daughter of the Samurai.* I remember crying during certain scenes not because I understood what went on but because Mrs. Sugimoto cried. Today, some forty years later, I know how moving Bunraku can be. The beauty of the language and the emotion in the voice of the narrator stir me. The range of the samisen, from deep warm tones to sharply percussive notes, provides an unusual musical experience—and this is the background for the startlingly human acting of the puppets on the Bunraku stage.

An unseen figure dashes across the stage pulling the curtain with him, revealing a daimyo's mansion. On a small platform on the right of the stage, the *tayū* (narrator), in formal Edo-period attire, kneels in front of an elaborate reading stand, and a samisen player at his side, similarly dressed, begins playing his instrument with a large plectrum. The tayū sets the mood with wordless intonation, then begins to recite the story. The expressionless musician plays in varying tempos, sometimes punctuating his notes with cries resembling grunts or yelps.

A black curtain is snapped open on the right and a puppet makes its measured entrance in response to the disciplined movements of three black-robed men. The doll is one-half to two-thirds life size and elaborately costumed.

At first you are aware of the three men who glide behind the doll. You notice how one man operates the puppet's head and right arm, another the left arm, and occasionally you see the masked head of the third, crouching as he moves the puppet's legs. Soon you cease to worry about how the three doll handlers work together—you simply see a living being that breathes, runs, and laughs. The puppet comes alive: the men attached to it fade into the background.

The narrator sets the scene to samisen accompaniment, describes the action and speaks all the parts—sometimes as many as eleven characters appear in one scene, ranging from a tiny child to a mean grandmother. The themes cover the gamut—loyalty, treason, adultery, honor, jealousy, star-crossed love, travel, tomfoolery, fantasy, and suicide among them. Some plays concern ancient heroes or famous incidents but the dilemmas facing the ordinary man when passion conflicts with obligation provide plots for most. In all the plays, it is the swing from the real to the unreal, the intensely moving to the absurd, the beautiful to the somber that gives Bunraku its unique flavor.

The combination of three different art forms that make up Bunraku is intriguing. Three independent elements—narration, music, and puppetry—create an artistic force of continually varying intensity and direction. The lines of communication between narrator and musician and puppeteer intersect at forever different angles. Thus, your attention is often shifted from the action on the main stage to the tayū and the samisen player and back again.

A reflection of the urban culture of the Edo period, Bunraku continues to live today as a many-faceted spectacle of sound, color, and movement.

Barbara C. Adachi

Kabuki, 歌舞伎

Kabuki theater.

Kabuki is a vivid example of an entire half of the Japanese arts that Westerners too often forget. It is vigorous, complex, flamboyant, colorful, and gutsy. Kabuki is more than a popular form of theater combining the various performing arts in a spectacle of great intensity. It is a way of life. To approach it simply as another theatrical performance is a mistake. Like life, Kabuki must be lived, inhabited, and enjoyed for its multiple array of sensual delights. Foreigners and young Japanese who complain that it is too long or too slow do not realize that, like life itself, Kabuki has its moments of repose as well as its climaxes.

The most striking image of the Kabuki experience came to me one day while I was sitting in the front row at the famous Kabukiza theater in Tokyo. As I turned to watch my favorite actor perform as a wicked magician on the *hanamichi*—the "flower path," or runway, that reaches from the stage out into the audience—my eye was caught by a little old lady sitting on the aisle just below the posturing actor, slowly peeling an orange. Here, I thought to myself, is Kabuki. Vicariously living the grandeur of the villain, that little old lady was seated comfortably at home eating an orange. The actor, too, was caught up in both dimensions, for the perfume of that orange no doubt rose straight to his nostrils.

This example illustrates the intimacy between actor and spectator and the fullness of sensual appeal that both belong to Kabuki. But above all the little lady reminds us that the three-hundred-year-old Kabuki experience is like a picnic. One need not remain perched tensely on the edge of one's seat (though there are occasional moments of spine-chilling effects and much grotesquerie), but can generally relax in familiar and comfortable surroundings, and enjoy the exhilaration of the exotic and the dramatic.

This side of Kabuki may not always be in evidence today, but if one studies old theater prints, the vendors delivering food and the spectators eating and drinking and even fighting are clearly visible. Today one can still buy a box lunch to enjoy during the

Onoe Baikō, Onoe Kikugorō, and Kawarazaki Gonjūrō in the Kabuki drama *Kurotegumi Kuruwa no Tatehiki.*

four- to six-hour performance. Even if you do not eat, there is still the shouting: howls of admiration and approval from the audience serve to further enhance intimacy with the actors. As the actor is thrown into the audience by the hanamichi, we throw ourselves at him through the cries echoing from way up in the galleries.

Kabuki's secret, in addition to its complex, highly elaborated art form, lies in this precious blend of the real and the unreal, the humble and the exotic, life and theater. It is a place where we can live out our wildest dreams while indulging in the most familiar daily routine.

Leonard C. Pronko

Nihonbuyō, 日本舞踊

Japanese dance.

My first memories of Japanese dancing go back to my childhood on our family ranch in Texas and a few figures painted on an imported tea set. As a graduate student at the University of Wisconsin, I had the chance to attend a course in which I learned to appreciate something of the richness of Japanese dancing, enough at least to draw me to Japan time and again to study the classic dance forms of *Bugaku,* Nō, Kabuki, and *Nihonbuyō.*

The story of the goddess Ame-no-Uzume dancing on an inverted wooden tub to lure the Sun Goddess, Amaterasu, out of her cave to enlighten the darkened world is to be found in Japan's oldest written document, the *Kojiki.* This Shinto religious dance, the *Kagura,* may be considered the mythical prototype of all Japanese dance–man's way of communicating with the gods.

Kanawa, danced by Takehara Han.

As a result of the evolution of Kabuki, the various traditions of Japanese dance that had existed prior to the seventeenth century were brought together. Thus Nihonbuyō blends the slow moving techniques of the Nō dance with the leaping and stomping of the more lively folk dances and the restrained, repetitious patterns of the Bugaku brought to the imperial court from China and Korea. These various elements in turn are bound together by mimetic elements that have helped make the Japanese dance the popular cultural art that it is.

Training in Nihonbuyō begins traditionally with the simple dances and proceeds to more complicated pieces as the student builds up a better vocabulary and understanding. The deeper one goes into these dances, the more one finds them a key to the rich resources of Japanese culture, its geography, history, morality, religion, myth, and ritual. The physical understanding and interpretation of this kinetic art furthers one's development of contained and expressed emotion. Both poetic sentiment and robust passion are expanded through the complex rhythms and technical control needed to perform the broad range of subject and idea captured in these dances. As a social refinement the study of Nihonbuyō opens the heart to traditional Japanese sensitivity. Performance leads to the core of realizing values of entertainment as deeply rooted social custom and art.

Of all the hand props used in the Japanese dance, the folding fan (*sensu*)–developed and perfected in Japan–is the most comprehensive. Its expressiveness begins with the preparatory stance and passes on to the simulation of natural phenomena (waves, rain, snow, flowers), cultural objects (sword, umbrella, saké cup, letter), and even to abstract metaphors. In the hands of an expert the fan can be tossed, flipped, and spun to perform feats of stunning impressiveness.

Though the aesthetic beauty and popularity of Nihonbuyō have carried it around the world, I find it continually bringing me back to Japan, where this timeless celebration of movement reflects not only the traditions from which it originated but the aspirations of a people growing into the twenty-first century.

Lonny Joseph Gordon

Shingeki, 新劇

A twentieth-century theatrical form; the new-drama movement.

It is early spring, 1945. The air raids over Japan have grown so intense that life in the major cities has become precarious. In a farmhouse deep in the mountains, we find a mother and her daughter-in-law who are among the thousands who have streamed into rural areas to escape the bombings. In this naturalistic setting, the interaction between these two women from Tokyo, a long-time friend of the daughter-in-law's husband (who is off to war), and a host of simple but lively local mountain folk forms the basis for Kinoshita Junji's well-known 1949 play, *Yamanami* (The Mountain Range).

As a typical example of Japan's *shingeki,* or new drama, this thoroughly contemporary play moves on several levels at the same time: a portrait of the frustrations of a young Japanese woman caught between the unyielding demands of the traditional family system, represented by her mother-in-law, and her inner life; a love story of the blossoming affection between a young man and his friend's wife; and a microcosm of the dilemma of modern Japan, longing for an irretrievable and idealized rural past.

I first saw *Yamanami* in the impressive revival staged by the noted Tokyo theatrical troupe Mingei in 1978. It made me realize that shingeki has arrived at the point that it can now reach back and retrieve native works of lasting quality.

Shingeki first evolved from a number of late-nineteenth-century endeavors to create a drama that would reflect the processes of Westernization and social change that characterized the Meiji era. Attempts to modernize Kabuki to this end had been unsuccessful. The subsequent drama of the *shinpa* ("new school")–which has survived to the present day–proved to be too sentimental and unsophisticated to fill the gap. The model for a modern theater for Japan came rather from the stimulus to modernization itself: the West. As early as the first decades of this century native playwrights were producing works in imitation of Western trends ranging from romanticism to left-wing social protest. And the staging

The Shingeki play *Yamanami,* performed by the Mingei Group.

of Western plays, everything from Greek tragedy to Beckett, was important from the first and has remained so to the present day.

Although shingeki has now become an established form of drama in Japan and has broken away from its former reputation as theater for intellectuals, it has not done so without a long and trying struggle. At present shingeki is flourishing, with some 164 troupes, of which 135 are centered in Tokyo. Some shingeki actors and actresses support their fame–and themselves–through television appearances; but a large number of dedicated artists continue to scrape along, much like their counterparts in the West. The final result is that the Japanese theatergoer, along with people like me, can enjoy a form of theater that truly reflects the various trends that make up modern life in Japan.

Robert Rolf

Naniwabushi, 浪花節

A kind of chanted ballad.

Among Japan's traditional balladeers, raconteurs, and epic storytellers, "these strange newcomers do not seem to fit in," observed a popular publication around 1830. "The story is recited and sung by one person, while someone else plays the samisen. Even more surprising, most of the story is actually spoken; the musical interludes are virtually independent."

In light of the difficult time that *naniwabushi* had shaking its unenviable reputation, it is not hard for us to read between the lines of the commentator's remarks: "What ill-bred offspring our balladeers have produced!" Even when naniwabushi did become an accepted genre late in the nineteenth century, some masters of the older *rakugo* and *manzai* traditions felt a sense of relief every time "that uncouth ranting" began one of its periodical declines. Some still do.

Naniwa is both one of the old names for Osaka, where this type of storytelling originated, and the family name of Isuke, a mid-eighteenth-century bard who introduced the style. *Bushi* means simply "tune." Long unable to compete for the more respectable soapboxes, the naniwa balladeers traveled around and lightened the life of the neighborhood with installments of their ever-expanding melodramas. A few rose to prominence in the Meiji era, the peak years of naniwabushi.

The urban environment of the late eighteenth century and after provided the ideal incubator for popular art forms, and naniwabushi skillfully exploited themes most appealing to mass tastes. Chivalry, power, and honor among thieves were among the best loved. For all the scorn they drew from the intelligentsia, the themes of the naniwabushi, like those of the Beatles of the 1960s, struck a chord with the sentiments of the common man. They reflected the anguish and passion of lovers, the guilt, the boredom, and the affections of husband and wife, the joys and trials of filial piety, and above all, the loyalty and deep attachment between a master and his disciples.

During the 1930s the art experienced another surge in popularity, but this time the values expressed in the lyrics were bolstered by a militant ideology that worked them into the ideal profile of the fighting man. As such, the naniwabushi episodes became an easy target for social and political progressives, and indeed the name itself has assumed connotations of the feudalistic, the irrational, the old-fashioned. But for all that, the ethos of naniwabushi lives on, in the same way that the Japanese people remain steeped in their traditional culture. The still popular *kayō-kyoku* songs and the style of their performers, for example, echo the naniwabushi in an almost uncanny fashion.

Naniwabushi is no longer a popular form today, since its stories and its values really do belong to the past. But they tell us a great deal about the kind of human relationships that still form the core of contemporary Japanese society.

Patricia Murray

Piano, ピアノ

The piano.

Japan now ranks among the world's leading exporters of quality pianos; and one out of every ten Japanese families owns one. Yet there is not even a Japanized word for this instrument from the West, such as the colorful Pidgin English term "big black bugger fight-em teeth."

"A piano is a piano is a piano," Gertrude Stein might have said. But not so in Japan. Here the piano has become something of a national craze, thanks to the postwar economic-recovery miracle.

In the Meiji and Taishō eras, it was only the elite who could afford pianos or who had space for one in their homes. Then, in the mid-1920s, it became the fashion for the nouveaux riches to have one Western room in their new Japanese-style houses. This room—seldom used except to entertain guests—was equipped with imported rugs, imitation fireplaces, stuffed chairs with antimacassars, bookcases crammed with translations of foreign classics, and the most noticeable token of wealth and culture of all: a shiny, black upright piano.

So it was that some fifty years ago the piano became a status symbol, and the seemingly unattainable dream of millions. But not everyone who bought pianos in those days had any great love for classical music. I recall from my Japanese childhood some neighbors who bought a piano. At first the piano top was merely covered with decorative lace on which was placed a vase with artificial flowers. These were shortly joined by a doll in a large glass case. And eventually the piano top became a jumble of books, dolls, photographs, and trophies. I believe my sister may well have been the only person who ever played that piano.

I am afraid things may not be greatly different today, when almost everyone can afford a piano. Except that now we have hundreds of thousands of boys and girls—mostly girls—taking lessons and banging away at the insistence of their mothers. The problem is that too few of these mothers are culturally equipped to provide more than the money for lessons, being preoccupied with soap operas on television, shopping sprees, and other time-killing pursuits of the modern, liberated Japanese housewife.

Japan has produced its full share of world-class concert pianists, it has excellent music conservatories, and thousands of Japanese have a genuine and informed appreciation of piano music. But these things do not account for the sale of more than two million pianos in the so-called piano-boom decade from 1965 to 1975. Such a phenomenon can only be attributed to sudden affluence and a compulsion to keep up with the Suzukis.

It certainly has little to do with real musicianship. Indeed, there is now much talk about "piano noise pollution." One enraged apartment dweller not long ago actually murdered the mother of a doubtful child prodigy in an argument over the incessant practicing next door. This well-publicized event may have triggered a decline in the popularity of the piano. Sales last year were down ten thousand from the year before.

Walter Nichols

Kangeiko, 寒稽古

Midwinter training for those in the martial arts.

In the old lunar calendar *shōkan,* the start of the coldest season of the year, was reckoned at fifteen days from the beginning of the twelfth month. Another fifteen days brought *daikan,* the great cold; and fifteen days after that, the first day of spring. In the new calendar daikan occurs on the twenty-second or twenty-third of January. But whatever system one uses, this period of intense cold has traditionally been adopted as a time of winter training by martial arts groups—what the Japanese call *kangeiko.*

During kangeiko extra sessions are scheduled, windows are thrown open, and training continues in the unheated and drafty hall. No clothing other than the standard uniform is allowed. Even this is not considered demanding enough, so that other and more severe practices are held outdoors. Running barefoot over the snow and training in frozen fields are favored by some, but it is probably *misogi*—meditation under a waterfall or in a river—that is the most famous of these winter practices. Karate groups will run to a waterfall, remove the tops of their uniforms, step over the ice, and stand under the fall. Legs apart, they thrust alternately with each fist, announcing each punch with a shout. The aikido group to which I belong does misogi in a river. Wearing small loincloths (*fundoshi*), we gather in a circle, run through special calisthenics to call forth our *ki,* or spiritual force, and then for ten minutes or so submerge ourselves up to our necks.

Misogi has its origins in Shinto and Buddhist practices. Even today in certain districts priests and lay people will gather on a sacred mountain for thirty days of winter austerities. In thin white robes and wearing straw sandals, they walk every night from village to village visiting shrines and temples, begging alms while beating drums and chanting the name of Buddha. During the day they sit in meditation, read scriptures, and purify themselves with misogi. On the final day a huge fire service is held to ensure that the prayers and austerities of the worshipers will be efficacious during the coming year.

Occasionally martial arts groups join such religious processions, but even if they do not, most will practice at least once a winter before a shrine or temple. Swordsmen and archers in particular prefer training at a shrine and often hold New Year's training on the first of January.

In most training halls it is not possible to advance to a higher rank if one avoids practice in winter or its summer equivalent, *natsugeiko,* training in the hottest time of the year. Despite its apparent severity, winter training is still done faithfully by martial-arts groups. Perhaps only one who has taken part in it can appreciate kangeiko for what it is: a test of endurance, a form of prayer for prosperity and health, and a method of purifying, brightening, and regenerating one's body and mind.

John Stevens

Jūdō, 柔道

The sport of judo.

"Strong in its softness is the wisteria spray; the pine in its hardness is broken by the weak snow." This basic principle of *jūdō*, taken from a text dating back many centuries, is but one of the hundreds of such verses in the martial traditions of Japan. They show the intellectual and artistic level of the samurai who authored them, so very different from the typical figures of Western chivalry.

The techniques of judo as an Olympic sport are well known, but they are only a small part of an original repertoire that had to be progressively narrowed to eliminate anything dangerous. This restriction has reduced the resources open to a small man; for instance, although he can now be held firmly by the collar, he may no longer attack his opponent's wrists. For this reason weight categories have had to be introduced. But even so, judo has far more scope for originality than any other sport and as such is also all the more valuable as a training for life.

Although *jūdō* literally means "the way of softness," this does not mean simple passivity. Imagine someone rushing at you as you stand on the edge of a cliff. If you are passive, or even if you resist, his momentum will carry you over the edge—unless you happen to be overwhelmingly stronger. But if, just before his outstretched arms reach you, you throw yourself abruptly at his feet, he will trip and go over in your stead. This is *jū*. It requires exact timing, rapid and precise movement of the whole body, and a calm spirit. The particular movement referred to here is called *yoko-sutemi* and is still in use today.

More than simply a collection of techniques and methods, judo embodies the sense of higher moral standards. What differentiates it from other sports is the spirit of decorum and discipline with which it pursues its final goal: not the conquest of an opponent in competition, but the overcoming of the weakness of one's own heart. That is what is meant by *dō*.

Judo goes far beyond self-defense. In fact, the student of judo

is expected to find skillful means of avoiding meaningless brawls, even if that means sacrificing his "status" by running away. When he must fight, he knows what to do; but he is taught to refrain from combat whenever possible.

Most of us, like the fellow on the cliff edge, are frequently hampered by the inability to part with our habits. The student of judo learns to make sudden, decisive, and total reversals, and to find original ways and means to meet new circumstances without being overawed by them. In this sense the principles learned on the judo mats reach out beyond the limits of martial artistry to spiritual, moral, and intellectual realms as well.

Trevor P. Leggett

Hyakunin-isshu, 百人一首

The card game using one hundred poems by one hundred poets.

Aside from the occasional group of card-playing students, the phenomenon of the spontaneously organized game of Monopoly or Crazy Eights or any of the other hundreds of parlor games so familiar to the West has almost no place in Japanese adult society. And television seems to be doing its best to prevent the popularity of such games among children from taking root and producing a generation of game-loving grown-ups. Like so many areas of Japanese life, games are compartmentalized according to status, sex, age, self-image, and season. Mah-jongg, *Go, Shōgi,* and *Hanafuda*

The twenty-third national Queen of Hyakunin-isshu title match, 1979.

all belong to a certain cultural pattern that seems to frustrate the notion of "fun for all ages, any time, anyplace."

The same can be said of the parlor game *Hyakunin-isshu,* which forms part of New Year celebrations throughout Japan. Although sometimes used by children to play games similar to Western card games, its two sets of one hundred cards, often elaborately drawn and usually stored in special lacquered cases, belong properly to the first days of the New Year. The two sets of cards are matched as the first and second parts of one hundred famous poems by one hundred famous poets. One person, designated as Reader (or "intoner"), shuffles and stacks a set of cards on which the poems are inscribed, while the remaining cards, containing only the closing lines, are spread out on the floor. As the Reader slowly begins to read from the first card he turns over, the Players—either competing individually for the whole field of cards, or teaming up in pairs to divide the territory—scramble about on the tatami to locate and lay claim to the match. The delightful incongruity of young and old, decked out in their New Year's best, falling over one another and flaying their arms about is all part of the fun. And even the serious and competitive spirit that has brought the game to the level of a national championship with an annual playoff televised on January second does not stop it from being the great humorous spectacle it is supposed to be.

The *Hyakunin-isshu* itself is a collection of poems dating from the seventh to the thirteenth century, probably edited by a court noble named Fujiwara no Teika. Although its sporting associations may hinder its literary reputation, there are many poems of considerable merit, worthy of the long tradition of the Japanese poetic *waka.* Consider just one example:

Nagakaran	
Kokoro mo shirazu	If he be true I'm unaware;
Kurokami no	But since the dawn saw him depart
Midarete kesa wa	As all disheveled is my hair,
Mono o koso omoe.	So in confusion is my heart.

As for me—in the company of those who can ferret out the matching card after hearing but a single syllable or two—I shall always feel the perpetual novice. But that, too, is part of the fun.

Noah S. Brannen

Mājan, 麻雀

Mah-jongg.

To the uninitiated, it is no easy matter to understand how the clitter-clatter of tiles and the intense concentration of four people seated about a table talking to themselves in a hybrid of esoteric Japanese and Chinese could have come to be one of the all-time great collective enthusiasms of modern Japan. But to those who know the game of Mah-jongg from the inside, the reasons are self-evident.

First played in the imperial courts of China some two hundred years ago, the game later spread to the common people among whom it became a national pastime. A U. S. resident of Shanghai, J. P. Babcock, coined the name Mah-jongg (meaning, the "old sparrow, spotted like the leaves of the jute") and carried the game to Europe, whence it found its way to America and turned into a parlor fad during the 1920s. As its popularity faded with the depression, the game traveled to Japan and took on new life. Clubs sprang up everywhere; a number of major associations were formed and rules were stabilized.

Originally Mah-jongg was played with some fifty cardlike *mā-chao* (which some still insist give the game its name), but these were later replaced with more serviceable tiles, or *pai,* made of bone, ivory, bamboo, and, most recently, plastic. Basically, Mah-jongg is a shirttail relation of rummy, involving the accumulation of triplets, runs, and a pair to complete a hand of fourteen tiles. The one hundred and thirty-six tiles, which are erected in a square wall from which they are distributed and drawn, are composed of four each of: three suits numbered from one through nine, three "dragons," and four "winds." A single round, or half-game, may take anywhere from one to two hours.

The secret of Mah-jongg's enchantment—of one game leading to another and another, often deep into the night—lies somewhere behind the popular saying, "seven parts luck, three parts skill." Many seasoned players are convinced they can reverse those odds. Others, more respectful of its wisdom, turn to deception, teaming

up to prey on the naive who occasionally wander into the parlors looking for a game. All of which makes more sense when one learns that Mah-jongg is in fact another of those unsanctioned forms of gambling that thrive in the cracks between the laws of Japan. Add to this the massive literature and lore surrounding the game, schools offering courses in its skills, and the incessant pressures of already addicted friends, and the lure of its spell becomes almost irresistible. With a marital-discord potential approaching that of the American football season, Mah-jongg can now claim an estimated two out of ten people–from teens to sixties, men and (in growing numbers) women–who frequent the parlors to "play Chinese."

James W. Heisig

Shinbun, 新聞

Newspapers.

The trouble with Japanese newspapers is that most people cannot read them—unless, that is, they are Japanese. They can and they certainly do. No other country in the world has a higher literacy rate than Japan, nor a higher rate of newspaper dissemination; nor, to underscore the matter that troubles us, as large and sophisticated a press that is so thoroughly indigenous.

But wait, that doesn't sound right. What can be more indigenous than the typical local newspapers found in other countries, especially the United States? They devote columns to the readers' own activities, such things as weddings and bridge parties, while their international news coverage is as meager as can be. Their prime aim is to "localize" everything, even foreign stories, for otherwise, it is said, nobody would read them.

With Japanese newspapers, however, the overriding rule and assumption for editing are precisely the opposite. News that the readers may be expected to know already is not covered, while very generous space is given to the serious developments in the world abroad. And the more "foreign" the flavor, the more appealing it is expected to be.

This may suggest a number of things, all of them likely true. One is that Japanese newspaper readers are intellectual, or at least they approach their newspapers in such a mood. They expect to *learn* something.

It is the major Japanese dailies—with circulations upward of ten million and thus ranking among the biggest in the world—that are the most serious. A most popular press, but not at all in the sense that term is usually intended. It won't compromise its dignity, notwithstanding occasional waxing of sentimentality over an appropriate story. For real titillation one must turn to a certain class of weekly magazines, to which the sensationalist journalism is relegated.

Another important characteristic of the Japanese press is the overwhelming preeminence of national newspapers, and here another comparison with American journalism has to be cited. It has already been made; we will only cite it.

In postwar Japan, the American instructors in democracy decided to rebuild the country's war-shrunken press by having grassroots newspapers sprout throughout the country. It was like trying to grow bamboo in Lapland. The Japanese preference for national newspapers shows the way they prefer to identify themselves; it is one of the most explicit manifestations of the homogeneous nation.

There is no room here for personalized journalism, either. Bylines are rare. Editorials are dry and objective, suffocated by the ubiquitous "on the other hand." Intimacy is never sought. As a result, although readers tend to be loyal, they don't love their newspapers. The idea would seem ridiculous. But neither do they complain.

Strange? That is what is so indigenous, you see.

Holloway Brown

Bungaku Zenshū 文学全集

Collected literary works.

Japan is a nation of bookstores. Large and small, they are found in virtually every neighborhood, and more often than not are packed with browsers. The Japanese publishing world pours forth an endless treasure of books on every topic imaginable, but perhaps the jewel of the industry is the *bungaku zenshū.*

Seldom containing what its name literally states ("complete literary works"), the bungaku zenshū is normally a large, multivolume literary anthology. Enter any good bookstore in Japan and you will see them, lined up in rows of neatly boxed books, covering the whole spectrum of literature—classic, modern, contemporary, Japanese, Chinese, and Western.

With the current costs of printing, the amount of capital needed to purchase a ten- or twenty-volume zenshū can be staggering for even the high-salaried Japanese businessman. One cannot but wonder who in the world buys these sets. Of course, libraries do, but the hundreds of bulky volumes taking up shelf space in the local bookstore are intended to catch the eye of the individual customer. Overwhelmed by such a massive accumulation of culture, he may decide against taking on the burden of monthly payments, but at least he will leave the store awe-struck. The bungaku zenshū are a mark of prestige for all concerned: for the publishing house that would be seen as discerning, for the bookstore that wants to appear to have everything, and for the individual owner investing in a massive block of culture.

There would be nothing uniquely Japanese about all of this were it not for the fact that these collections are published on such a surprisingly large scale and are made so conspicuous. One reason for the abundance of books, bookstores, and private collections is the obvious shortage of lending libraries in Japan. Another is the success of the Japanese at marketing education and culture as consumer items. This is an industry ranging from such traditional favorites as the tea ceremony and flower arrangement to samisen picking and English-conversation lessons. And behind all

this activity there seems to lie a strong and innate belief in the need for constant self-improvement—the lingering philosophical influence of the earlier Spartan samurai ethic.

Robert Rolf

Kinen-shashin, 記念写真

Commemorative photographs and snapshots; souvenir snapshots.

As a student at Berkeley, I enjoy studying out on the sloping lawns that skirt the campanile to soak up the California sun, browse through my class notes, and eye the streams of Japanese tourists washing across the campus. In the eyes of these pilgrims, arrived at one of the bastions of American education, I imagine myself, with all due modesty, a fair representative of the student type they have come to see. Sunning oneself half-naked in public while studying is certainly a custom that has not taken root in Japan (and not only because there are so few lawns to sprawl out on). But to my surprise, I have yet to be photographed by any of the tourists. They are too busy taking pictures of one another standing in front of the campanile.

People the world over commemorate outings, special events, and the stages of life with pictures, but surely few do it with such enthusiasm and sense of purpose as the Japanese. Everywhere, at home and abroad, you can see them posed in front of some monument, plaza, or scenic spot for a snapshot to record their visit. Indeed it seems as if an essential part of every famous landmark and panoramic scene in Japan is the enterprising cameraman awaiting the busloads of tourists who would not feel that they had truly "seen" the place unless they could return home with proof to "be seen." And of course, there are those more formal occasions that also require commemorative photos: a baby on its first visit to the local shrine, the wedding-ceremony couple, a graduating high-school class, a special visitor to one's home, and so on.

The practice of recording for posterity a gathering or visit is not a purely contemporary phenomenon that came with cameras. In former times the Japanese had other ways of commemorating special events. Medieval and early modern poets, for example, would preserve an event by composing rounds of linked verse. And travelers to the country's scenic spots—places made famous, in the days before picture post cards, by the flood of verses celebrating their beauty—could say that they, too, had "been there" by

composing their own poetic "snapshots" to be recited later when tales of travel were to be told. To be sure, such literary efforts tended to mediocrity, but not nearly so much as their modern photographic equivalents. By making themselves the focus of their pictures, rather than aiming at objective composition, contemporary Japanese tourists take the poetry out of their photographs. And as for the tourists to Berkeley, I'm beginning to think I should change my strategy for getting into some snapshot as the prototypical American student. I could try my luck in front of Sproul Hall. . . . But no, on second thought, that wouldn't work either. Not that there aren't plenty of tourists milling around, but the only thing that seems to get into their photos, as far as I can tell, is Sproul Hall—and, of course, their companions.

Edward Fowler

Eigo
エイゴ
English.

Nearly a century ago Basil Chamberlain opened his famous essay "English as She is Japped" with the sentence: "English as she is spoke and wrote in Japan forms quite an enticing study." We might well say the same thing today. Despite the tremendous effort and investment put into foreign-language teaching, Japan still abounds in the "Japlish" that Chamberlain found so entertaining.

Three years of English is obligatory in most junior high schools, followed by three more years in senior high school, and usually continuing for another two years for those attending university. But with all that, few Japanese—including those who end up as English teachers—can converse freely in the language or write it with any degree of proficiency. English, or more correctly *Eigo,* is taught as an academic exercise with so much attention to memorizing fine points of grammar and vocabulary that it ceases to be a means of communication. The examinations for which these methods prepare the student are in turn prepared by those who have gone through the same system, with the result that they do not test linguistic ability but merely the capacity to memorize relatively disconnected bits of information.

This situation becomes all the more ironic when one recalls that, despite the miseducation in English, thousands of English words have entered the Japanese language itself over the past few generations. Some of these loanwords represent new concepts for which there were no equivalents, or at least none that caught on, in Japanese itself. *Terebi* ("television") is an example. Others have rendered the old Japanese synonyms archaic, as *rabu-retaa* ("love letter") did to *koibumi.* Still others coexist with Japanese words of the same meaning, such as *tsuma* and *mai waifu* ("my wife"). Occasionally the foreign word carries a special meaning distinguishing it from the older Japanese word, as *raisu* (rice eaten on a plate with a fork) is differentiated from *gohan* (rice eaten in a bowl with chopsticks). Many English loanwords get new, restricted meanings in Japanese. Thus *mishin* ("machine") always means sewing machine.

Perhaps the most difficult class of all for the native speaker to recognize is the words that are abbreviated much the same way that the Japanese abbreviate their own Chinese compounds. *Zenesuto* ("general strike") and *sabu-naado* ("subterranean promenade," i.e., an underground walkway) are two of them. Finally, some words are not standard English at all, but new inventions of the Japanese, such as *sarariiman* ("salary man"), which means a white-collar worker.

What helps to keep this Eigo from becoming English is that the words are written in the limited sound system of the Japanese syllabary, which produces pronunciations totally unrecognizable to the native ear. At the same time it retards the efforts of the Japanese to learn to speak English intelligibly. On the positive side, these loanwords have helped the Japanese to cope with the demands of an international, technological world. Perhaps in the same way that English, as Anglo-Saxon, was enriched and beautified—by Greek, French, and Latin—Japanese can hope to be improved by its contact with English. But for the moment at least, these hopes belong clearly to the future.

Beverley D. Tucker

Kanji, 漢字

The Chinese ideograms used in writing Japanese.

Nothing is so surprising about the Japanese language than that, although it has fewer sounds than most other languages, it is bound to a system of writing that is one of the most complex to be found anywhere on earth. Nothing, perhaps, but the fact that Japan can boast a rate of virtually one hundred percent literacy.

Lacking their own script, the Japanese took over the ideograms, or *kanji,* as part of their response to the waves of Korean and Chinese monks carrying Buddhism to Japan from the fourth to the seventh century. At first restricted to use in classical Chinese texts, the kanji were later adapted to Japanese as well. This meant additional pronunciations and a distinct set of highly stylized characters to indicate grammatical inflections lacking in Chinese. This syllabary, the *kana,* was used for a brief period by the literati in place of the kanji, but by the fifteenth century the two had been fused firmly into a single system.

Under pressure from the occupying forces, Japan's postwar Ministry of Education selected 1,850 kanji (from the some 50,000 available) for general use. But this list, revised several times since, has hardly had the desired effect of promoting the elimination of kanji altogether. The average college graduate still reads over 3,000 characters.

Perhaps the best way to describe the system is through Arabic numerals, whose pronunciation depends on their context and the tongue of the person reading them. The simple shape 2 is read "two" in English–but not always. Shift the context and the sound changes as well: 20, 12, 1/2, 2nd. Multiply this by two thousand, add the complexity of form necessary to differentiate many times that number, and you have some idea of what every Japanese schoolchild is required to learn between the first and ninth grade.

While it has not kept all foreigners away, the "kanji curtain" certainly insulates Japan from many a well-wishing student of its culture, and at the same time has often enough become a rallying point for nationalistic backlashes. The choice of kanji over the

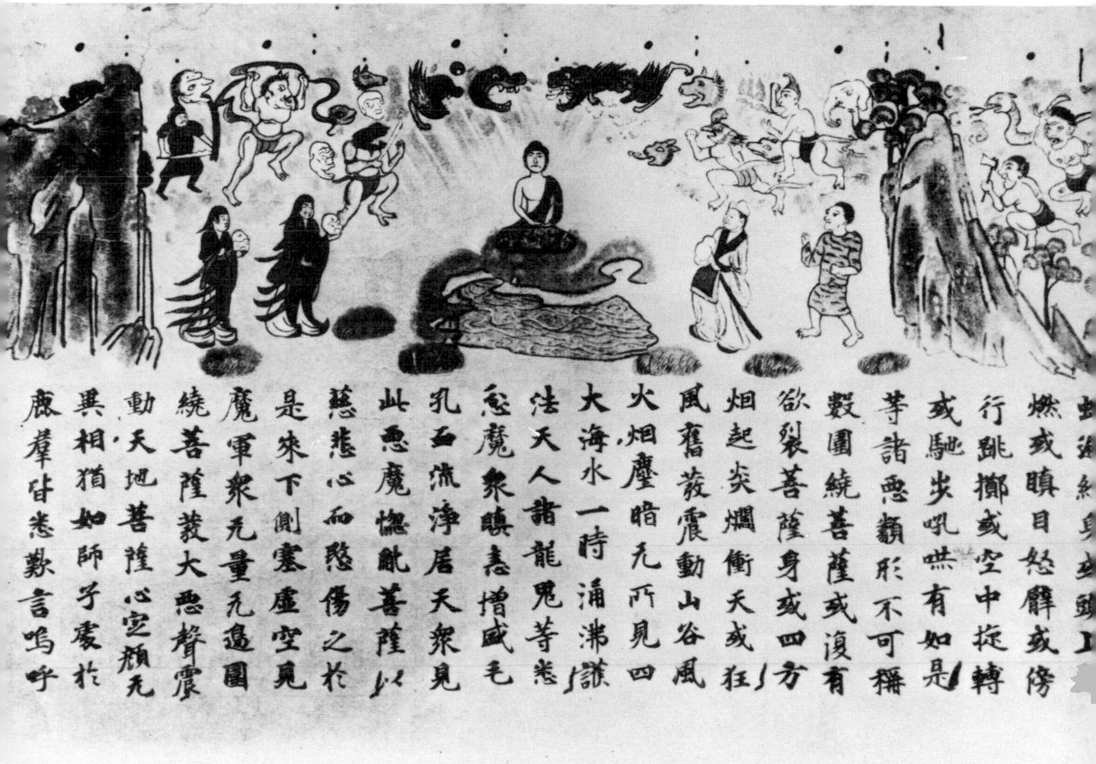

A section of an eighth-century sutra scroll from the collection of the Kyoto temple Daigo-ji. (National Treasure.)

alphabet, which Professor Edwin O. Reischauer has called "perhaps the greatest single misfortune in the history of Japan," makes us wonder whether all the soul squeezed into the ideograms might not have been preserved for posterity in some more communicable way. On the other hand, research conducted outside Japan has suggested that the minds of children can grasp meanings through the kanji with greater speed and comprehension than when forced to pass through a system of phonetics. And that makes us wonder if this ancient system of writing might not well be ages ahead of our benighted alphabets.

James W. Heisig

Giseigo, 擬声語

Onomatopoeia.

If you have never before met the following Japanese words, it might be fun to try to match them with their English equivalents. Which is which?

buu-buu	oink-oink	*gararito*	clattering
wan-wan	bow-wow	*pika-pika*	flashing
guu-guu	snoring	*sassato*	quickly

I won't ask how many you were able to get, but if you have come across them before you knew at once that the two columns already match.

The Japanese language is full of such words as these, and they help to make descriptions very concrete and vivid. They fall more or less into two groups: one describing sounds (*giseigo*) and the other describing quality or manner (*gitaigo*). Unlike their English counterparts, which can be verbs, nouns, or adverbs, Japanese onomatopoeic words function largely as adverbs.

Insofar as language is a direct indicator of cultural traits, Japanese's large glossary of onomatopoeic expressions for the sounds of wild birds and insects, and for natural phenomena like falling rain or snow, can be said to reflect the people's sensitivity to the natural elements. Particularly interesting is that words of this sort related to the sense of touch are far more numerous than those related to taste and smell. This brings to mind the comment of the modern Japanese scholar Itasaka Gen, who called the Japanese a *shokkaku minzoku*—a tactile race. It was said that during EXPO '70, the Japanese people were especially conspicuous for their tendency to handle the exhibits. Or again, a few months ago, during an exhibition in Tokyo of prehistoric fossils, a special dinosaur fossil was put out on display for visitors to touch, and those who had done so were awarded a certificate to show their friends.

In classical Japanese literature, onomatopoeic words are scarce, but it is doubtful that this reflects the actual usage of such words in the past. Linguistic usage, of course, differed according to age, status, and region. Since classic literature belonged to the works of the upper strata and occasions for use of such words are much fewer in literature, it is natural that their use in the common, spoken language would be quite different. On the theory that onomatopoeia is more common in primitive languages, the question arises whether this classifies Japanese as primitive. But here we must recall that, from ancient times down to the present, several cultures have coexisted within Japanese society, and a large number of old words have survived in the established language.

The unique characteristic of giseigo and gitaigo is that their minute differences of nuance correspond to the differences that distinguish one animal from another or one state of nature from another. For instance, rain can be described in Japanese as *potsun-potsun* (a drop here, a drop there), *potsu-potsu* (a few drops here, a few drops there), *shito-shito* (a steady, gentle drizzle) or *zaa-zaa* (cats and dogs)—to mention but a few of the possibilities. The more one learns of these idiomatic frills that find their way into the everyday conversations of the Japanese, the more deeply one comes to understand these people and their language.

Helen Yeung

Kappa, 河童

A mythical water imp.

Some Western readers of Akutagawa Ryūnosuke's famous allegorical novel *Kappa* must have wondered at the rich imagination of a modern author who could create such a strange creature. An imaginary animal he may be, but to the Japanese he is both very ancient and very familiar. A good swimmer is still called *kappa oyogi,* the common pageboy hairstyle is known as *okappa,* and "the easiest thing in the world" becomes in Japanese *kappa no he* ("a kappa's fart").

A look at some of the names given the kappa attests to the wealth of folklore surrounding him: "he who slips out of wells," "water tiger," "river urchin," "steed-puller," "arse-puller," and so on to no less than seventy different names for something that doesn't exist in reality.

What do kappas look like? As some of the names suggest, they are a bit like monkeys or small boys, with short-cropped heads and webbed feet and hands. They average about three to four feet high and weigh from twenty to forty pounds. Their faces often resemble a tiger's, and their skin is often horny but can change color like a chameleon's. An important characteristic of the kappa is the oval, dishlike hollow on top of his head in which he carries water. Should the water be spilled, he loses his strength—which is why the Japanese say that the best way to defeat a kappa when challenged to a test of physical strength is to open the contest with a bow: if the kappa returns it, he spills the water.

Despite his usual preference for horses, the occasional kappa will drag a human being under water—whence the name "arse-puller." But why pull by the bottom? Well, besides cucumbers (a few of which floated down the river can do wonders to appease an irate kappa), their favorite food is human liver which, it is said, they can slip out through the rectum. One farmer even made a pact with a kappa, providing his children with moxa marks on their buttocks so the kappa would know which ones to avoid. Many a story is told of women doing laundry by the river and the froggy, cold hand of the kappa reaching out to pat their bottoms. Some women were even believed to have borne a kappa's child.

The kappa is not entirely a figment of imagination, however; he is a living memory of the ancient realities and old beliefs of a race for whom water was especially needed for survival. There was a time when the material spirit of creation dwelt in water, the source of all things, and when the god of water (*suijin-sama*) ruled the underwater kingdom. The kappa is not only a delightful recollection of this water god, but also proof that the Japanese people still respect the forces that fashioned them and their culture.

Anthony V. Liman

Tanuki, 狸

The raccoon-dog.

That place of honor in the suburban garden that in America is held by the plastic flamingo and by the plaster gnome belongs to a far more interesting creature in Japan: the ceramic raccoon-dog, or *tanuki.* Of course, we do him injustice to translate his name as raccoon-dog, and not simply for reasons of scientific inaccuracy. He is no mere beast; he is one of the more magical figures of Japanese folklore.

In the Kabuki theater the tanuki reveals perhaps his most impressive talent, as well as his tragic flaw. He can transform himself into an irresistibly handsome young man, yet somehow his efforts at seduction never quite succeed. For even when he has thoroughly charmed some young lady, she always seems to retain enough good sense to put him to the test. So overpowering is the tanuki's fondness for saké that the mere scent of it causes his tail, until then well hidden under a stylish kimono, to rise. And so when the lady offers him a drink, he is exposed as a fraud and his deceit rendered harmless.

The tanuki of the children's story *Kachikachiyama* kills the old lady who sets him free, transforms himself into her double, and feeds her to her husband for dinner. Even so, the reader feels a little sorry for him when it is seen how easily, and cruelly, he is punished by a rabbit of only average intelligence.

In popular legend the tanuki shows a still more mysterious side. On nights when the full moon shines he and his companions gather in the forest and beat out strange rhythms on their bellies. There is no doubt about it: the sounds have been positively identified, even though no one has actually seen the rite. He has memorable physical attributes as well. His scrotum is reputed to cover an area equal to that of eight tatami mats and, if we are to believe the song, makes a prodigious sound when swaying in the wind. On the other hand, the tanuki is said to deserve credit for contributing to the art of calligraphy in Japan—by providing the hair for the writing brushes of the early ninth-century priest and calligrapher Kūkai.

All in all the tanuki emerges as a deceptively complex figure: possessed of magical powers but deprived of their full benefit by basic flaws; deceitful yet humorously inept at executing his schemes; not really dangerous like the fox, but not all that lovable either. How such a character achieved apotheosis in the suburban garden is something of a mystery. Certainly not through deceit, for his ceramic form tells it all: a knowing smirk on his face, a grossly protruding belly, scrotum reaching the ground, and a large jug of saké carried in full view. Whatever his faults, however, he is engaging company—far more so than the flamingo and the gnome. And it is a good thing he is available in clay, since the real tanuki is now near extinction.

Thomas J. Harper

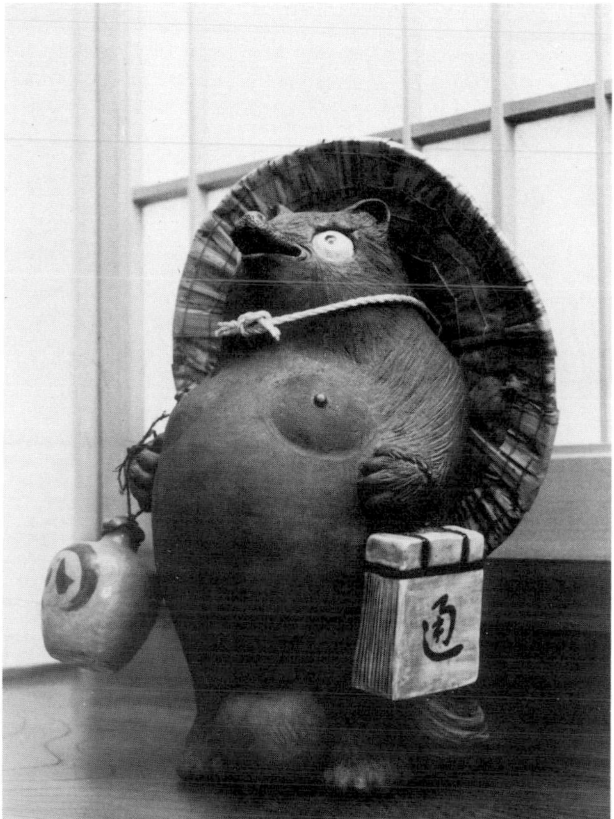

Hé, 屁

The fart.

Though the fart is, obviously, not a phenomenon to be observed uniquely in Japan, the Japanese attitude toward it is, I think, unique. Among indications of this attitude is that both *he* and its slightly more common variant, *onara,* are accepted. Both, for example, are found in Japanese dictionaries; one usually searches in vain, however, for "fart" in English dictionaries. In addition, the terms are heard in conversation with a frequency much greater than that with which (until recently) one encountered the like words in the West. Also, these are not considered dirty words and no euphemism ("break wind") is found necessary.

Many also are the proverbs–indications of a general acceptance. *"Aitsu wa furo no naka de he o hitta yō na yatsu da,"* for the translation of which Kenkyusha priggishly offers only: "He is a wishy-washy sort of fellow." Or, more philosophically: *"Hyaku nichi no seppō–he hitotsu,"* "An hour may destroy what took an age to build," advises Kenkyusha. English must content itself with, I believe, just one: "That is not worth a fart in hell." It is noted that both cultures use the fart in a derogative manner, but how much more the Japanese have to be disparaging with.

Finally, there is the common incidence of the fart in Japanese literature and the arts. While we in the West had had to content ourselves with but one celebrated fart (that of the frivolous seducer in Chaucer), the Japanese have long had the widest choice.

From the celebrated farting-contest scroll and the early illustrated *He Gassen* (The Fart Battle), up to such recent representations as the delightful farting games in Ozu Yasujirō's *Ohayō* (1959), Japan's culture is filled with vivid examples. To choose from poetry one need turn only to the *senryū,* that accepting form that, as R. H. Blyth so finely phrased it, is opposed to haiku in that "senryū are expressions of moments of vision into, not the nature of things, but the nature of man."

Farting is certainly included in the nature of man and there are a number of moments that capture this very human vision. One is:

The Edo-period scroll painting *He Gassen* (The Fart Battle), Reprinted from Richard Lane, *The Early Shunga Scroll* (Tokyo: Gabundō, 1979).

" 'And what may you all / Be laughing at, may I ask?' / The retired master's fart." And other is: "Four or five people, / Inconvenienced / By the horse farting / On the ferryboat." Concerning this last, Blyth, (whose translations the above are) says ". . . an extremely vulgar affair . . . the senryū writer, however, will and must have it and keep it, and bring it out again. Such things are among the miseries of life, and should be recorded as such."

Just here, I think, is the difference in attitude between Japan and the West. That a thing *is* is sufficient to warrant its notice, even its celebration. The hypocrisy of the idealistic (where some things, often those most intimately human, are to be denied) has not until recently infected Japan.

In both cultures the fart is funny but only in Japan, I think, is its humanity acknowledged. This entails a full acceptance of the human state. There is even a rubric for such matters. This is known as the *ningen-kusai* (literally, "smelling of humanity") and within it the *he* takes an honorable place.

Donald Richie

Daruma, だるま

Bodhidharma dolls.

Whatever it is about human nature that makes legend so much more appealing than hard fact, the Japanese have more than their share of it. Every Japanese schoolchild knows about the Indian monk called Bodhidharma who is credited with founding Zen Buddhism in China in the sixth century; but his objective history is no match for the tall tales that have made the familiar figure of the *Daruma* so beloved a part of the corporate imagination of Japan.

As the story goes, Daruma came to enlightenment after sitting in meditation facing a cave wall for nine years, without so much as moving or blinking his eyes. This latter detail becomes a bit easier

to swallow if one recalls that earlier, irritated at himself for dozing off, he had cut off his eye lids and cast them to the ground. The first two tea plants of China grew up on the spot—which is why, it is said, Zen monks even today drink tea to keep awake during meditation. At any rate, the effect of all this *zazen* (seated meditation) was that Daruma's legs fell off from disuse. And so it is that statuettes of Daruma in Japan depict him as a round, stern-faced, legless, bright red ball whose head blends directly into his shoulders without bothering to go through the usual convention of a neck. The mutilation is frequently rounded off by depriving him of arms as well—probably under the influence of the legend of the monk Hui K'o, who cut off his arms to demonstrate the seriousness of his intentions in following the way of Daruma.

"Seven times pushed over, eight times it rises" goes the proverb about Daruma, whose unmistakable roly-poly shape has made his name the perfect metaphor for everything from potbellied stoves and snowmen to the rounded bottle of Suntory Old whisky and (somewhat less honorably) a busy low-class prostitute. Add a little slot in the back, and the Daruma doll becomes the archetypal Japanese piggy bank. Political candidates in Japan customarily open election day by painting a black pupil into the white of one of Daruma's eyes. The winner, who has survived the ups and downs of the polls, is then entitled to paint in the other eye as part of the victory celebration—"both eyes open" being a Japanese idiom for success. In the same way, those subject to the rise and fall of the business world will procure a Daruma doll at the end of the year and paint in one eye as preparation for the New Year.

To keep Japan supplied with Daruma of sufficient apotropaic power, there are temples *(Daruma-dera)* that specialize in their production, and each New Year's there are the annual Daruma markets where old statues can be brought for ceremonial burning and new ones purchased in exchange.

Some day if you happen to catch little children playing that universal game of staring each other down until one of them laughs, listen closely and you might even catch the ditty that goes along with it in Japan, honoring the undisputed master of the art: *"Daruma-san, Daruma-san, niramekko shimashō."*

Karl Manougian

Ise, 伊勢

A famous Shinto pilgrimage site.

Ise is the site of the chief shrines of the Shinto religion, and as such it has been the object of pilgrimages by many centuries of Japanese. The shrine buildings are situated in a kind of park along the shallow but beautifully clear Isuzu River. They are approached over gravel walks bordered by cryptomerias. Not even the devastating typhoon of 1959, which felled many of the tallest trees, could alter the grandeur of such surroundings.

There are two main shrine buildings, the Inner and the Outer, dedicated respectively to Amaterasu, the Sun Goddess, and

Toyouke, the Goddess of Harvests. In keeping with a tradition that goes back to A.D. 690, the buildings are totally "renewed" every twenty years. An exact copy of the old edifice, made of the same materials, is erected a short distance away, and at the great ceremony known as *sengū,* or transference of the shrine, the divinity is moved from its old residence to a new one. Some months after the divinity has entered the new shrine, the old one is dismantled.

In contrast to Buddhist architecture, which attains its dignity from its age, these shrines look best when they are new. In them one can see clearly the peculiar Japanese genius for enabling materials to reveal their undisguised natures. The pillars and beams of magnificent wood are polished to satiny smoothness but not painted; every immaculate strand of reed in the thatched roofs is flawlessly aligned; the metal ornaments at the ends of the beams gleam with strength; each crossbeam fits securely into the pillars it joins without the use of nails—a perfect combination of the unadorned beauty of the natural object and the shaping hand of man.

In the past, especially during the Edo period, when people were constrained not only by edicts but by inflexible codes of conduct, secret visits to Ise were among the few permitted escape valves. In some years such visits became a national craze, and tens of thousands of people went singing and dancing along the roads to the great shrines. Ise's reputation as the "homeland of the heart," *kokoro no furusato,* for the Japanese was established long before the term came to be used commercially to attract tourists.

The chief attraction of the city of Ise used to be its licensed quarters—among the largest and most opulent in Japan. Many a young man celebrated his coming of age by visiting the shrines, worshiping, and then passing the night at one of the town's establishments. Times and circumstances have changed things, and today the town is not much more than a place to buy souvenirs.

The magnetism of Ise is perhaps greater today than ever before, not because of any increase in religious fervor, but because of the contrast its serene beauty provides with the surroundings in which most Japanese are now obliged to live.

Donald Keene

Zazen, 座禅

Zen meditation.

In a dim hall lighted by flickering candles, still figures face the faintly luminous wall. Outside in the pale of the morning a solitary robed figure stands poised to release a heavy wooden beam against the temple bell and break the silence with its slow resonances. The early morning period of *zazen* is coming to its end, but its spirit will continue throughout the activities of the day–walking, eating, working, studying. For more than merely sitting cross-legged in meditation, zazen is an attitude toward life that aims at an awareness of the subtlety and uniqueness of each moment.

Zen is one of the many traditions of Buddhism in Japan that are based on training and teaching through meditation. Within Zen itself differences in method distinguish the two best known sects, Rinzai and Sōtō, both of which developed in China and were carried to Japan within a generation of each other in the early thirteenth century by Eisai and Dōgen respectively. The teachings of Rinzai Zen encourage the concentration of one's mind on a single thing until it gradually comes to be emptied of all its conventional meanings. Devices called kōan–spiritual riddles–lead the student from stage to stage until enlightenment is reached.

By contrast, the techniques of Sōtō, as I can tell you from experience, tend to be bewildering to the beginner, alternately too formalistic and too formless. The stress is laid as much on one's behavior outside the meditation hall as within it. Indeed Dōgen himself composed a vade mecum for the Zen life that detailed behavior right down to one's toilet habits. But no activity is regulated without a purpose. In Sōtō temples, students are taught to assume the lotus position (legs crossed with soles facing upward on opposite thighs, back straight, chin tucked in, the top of the head as though reaching toward the ceiling) and to become the Buddha. Surprisingly enough, in contrast to Rinzai Zen, the word "enlightenment" is rarely mentioned in the Sōtō sect. Priests shy away from the expression and discourage students from setting it as a goal. Instead they speak of a "mindfulness" that should per-

meate all the things of life so that each activity can be experienced to the full, without distraction. When sitting, one should just sit; when eating, just eat; when bathing, just bathe. The minutely detailed rules—even the position of the chopsticks in eating is determined—are designed to liberate the mind from physical actions and allow it to fix on the activity itself.

In zazen the mind neither controls nor rejects. Thoughts flow in and out freely without being clung to or grasped at. The difficulties of meditating without an object of meditation, without a goal to be reached, are many. Yet for one who follows this way of doing rather than thinking about doing, the liberating zazen mind comes slowly, imperceptibly, to transform the things of life.

Gaynor Jenke

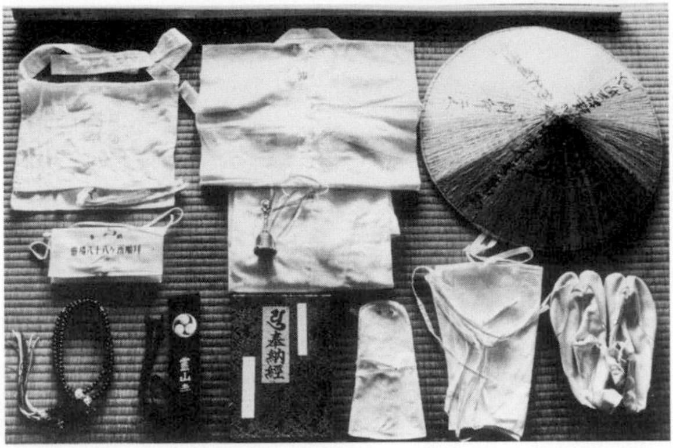

O-henro, お遍路

Pilgrimages.

Unless one has experienced the traditional Buddhist pilgrimage with its circuit of holy places, one doesn't really know what the word *o-henro* means in Japan. For the tourist in a hurry to get an overall view of a traditional circuit of thirty-four sacred sites, a special excursion from Chichibu (about ninety minutes northwest of Tokyo) has been organized recently that will take him the whole route, by bus, in a single day. In fact, chances are that most foreign tourists, who do not read the banners and posters left by pilgrims to the various temples, will even fail to notice that they are numbered and belong to the circuit at all. The most famous of these circuits is known as the *Hachijū-hakkasho* (the "eighty-eight sites") on the island of Shikoku. The organized tour takes about twelve days, averaging seven or eight temples a day.

For me, the most impressive moment of o-henro is when a group of elderly people—women usually outnumbering men—fully garbed in white, with stoles and cone-shaped hats, moves up the steep steps to the temple, staves in hand, to the accompaniment of the tinkling bells attached to their waists.

Some of these temples are consecrated to Kannon, others to the historical Buddha Shakyamuni, to Amida (the celestial Buddha), or to Yakushi (the healing Buddha). In front of the main hall the pilgrim sings, probably without understanding all the words, the shortest known sutra, called the *Hannya-shingyō.* Once inside the hall dedicated to Kōbō Daishi (the early ninth-century priest revered as the "Great Master of the Propagation of the Law"), one repeats the few syllables of a sacred invocation that is more easily understood: *namu* (blessed) *daishi* (Great Master) *henjō* (who illumines our way) *kongō* (to the Diamond World).

Meanwhile, so as not to waste any time, the bus driver and his assistants have rushed off to another place, where the priest and his wife, or persons hired for the task, are busy stamping the commemorative books of the individual pilgrims.

This is the way the pilgrimage is carried out today, with the help of modern transportation. Does this mean that the ancient spirit of individual pilgrims moving on foot for three months or more has disappeared? I think not. Of course, the arduous physical trial of the pilgrimage has largely gone, but the faith in the hearts of the people remains unchanged. I recall recently coming to a small restaurant, only to find that it had already closed. But the old lady, quick to recognize the face of a pilgrim, invited me in and made me supper free of charge. On another occasion, a farmer's wife gave me a ride in her husband's car, explaining, "It is not I, but the *O-daishi-sama* [Kōbō Daishi] himself who invites you." As long as such understanding survives, the spirit of the O-daishi-sama lives and continues to shower blessings on those who honor his memory.

Paul Reitsch

Butsudan
仏壇
The Buddhist family altar.

Anyone fortunate enough to be invited into a Japanese home will probably notice in one corner of the living room—or perhaps off in a small adjoining room—something that looks like an open closet with elevated platforms on several levels, on which are placed Buddhist images, copies of Chinese sutras, framed pictures, and other assorted religious articles. This is the *butsudan,* or Buddhist family altar, a miniature replica of the huge and elaborate altars enshrining Buddhist images that form the centerpieces of temples all over the land.

Photographs of ancestors and deceased family members are a prominent feature of the family altar, and are placed there as objects of veneration. For in Japan the deceased are referred to as *hotoke-sama* ("Buddha") and are considered to have entered the realm of the sacred. Through their enshrinement the oft-noted oriental trait of profound reverence for ancestors is given concrete expression, at the same time as their continued remembrance on the part of the living is ensured. It is not unusual for members of a pious family to regard those displayed on the altar as actually present, silent participants in the daily life of the family.

As a more direct sign of veneration, one will join hands in a respectful *gasshō* position, perhaps sounding the small bell placed in front of the altar, and enter into silent, commemorative prayer before the image of the ancestors. In addition, incense is lighted and offerings of flowers and food are placed on the altar. These are kept fresh and replaced regularly, reflecting the changes in season. Thus *o-mochi* (pounded-rice cake) is commonly found on the butsudan during the New Year season, as is some token of the fruits of the season.

The practice of keeping a Buddhist altar in the home dates back to early times, though it is difficult to assign a precise date. In the eighth-century chronicle *Nihon Shoki* we read: "In every home of every land, let there be a *bussha*." This small, detached house for the image of the Buddha was later moved indoors to a special room called the *butsuma*. Out of this developed the butsudan as we know it today.

Although the butsudan are more common in private homes than in apartments, it is not rare to find precious space in cramped quarters given to an elaborate altar. Money seems to be no object either; the simplest altars begin at around five hundred dollars, with the more ornate ones running into the thousands. Most first-class department stores will feature a display of altars and accouterments for sale, though the long tradition of craftsmanship associated with them still belongs to the small family shops to be found throughout Japan.

In a highly secularized modern society, the butsudan remains another of those signs of contradiction for which Japan is famous: a living vestige of ancient religious sentiment and traditional values.

Ruben Habito

Rokudōsen, 六道銭

The coins necessary to pay one's passage into the next world.

The custom of supplying the dead with money before burying them is common to many cultures of the world, ancient and modern. The Greeks used to slip a single obol into the mouth of the deceased, reckoning that this would serve as fare for the voyage across the river Styx. Hence, the old proverb, "Without money, even death is impossible." The Chinese used paper money. And one can still see Koreans stuffing the mouths of their deceased with rice and money, proclaiming, "Here are a hundred coins, here a thousand, here ten thousand!" It is said that the money will be needed for their trip to the other world.

In Japan, the dead are given three, six, seven, or forty-nine coins—depending on the region—which are put in a beggar's bag (*zudabukuro*) and hung about the neck of the corpse when it is laid in the coffin. Here, too, the claim is that the money is to be used to cross the river Sanzu, on whose opposite bank lies the land of the hereafter.

The story of the river Sanzu comes from a Japanese Buddhist sutra, the *Jizō-bosatsu Jūōkyō,* dating back to the Heian period. Therein it is stated that the dead must cross the river either on a bridge (if they have led a sinless life), through a ford (if they have committed only light offenses), or in the middle of the stream. The notion of a boatman, which is not found everywhere, is of later origin and seems to have spread through oral tradition.

According to another version, the *rokudōsen*—which means literally, "a penny to the six worlds"—is said to have been a kind of propitiatory fee. This popular belief goes back well before inheritance laws and seems to have continued on even after them. Traditionally in Japan, death is believed to bring about certain ritual interdictions. Among them is the taboo that binds the deceased's inheritance. Only if the money is "liberated" through a few token coins tossed into the tomb can the inheritors use the money after the burial without fear of harm.

"Even the judgments of hell depend on money" goes the saying in Japanese. Not only does this proverb criticize the influence of money in this world, but it also shows that their fear of the great ruler of the underworld was balanced with a bit of sarcasm—and also seen is the spirit of resignation with which the Japanese face life after death.

Jean Esmein

Mu, 無

Nothingness.

Yado no haru — A hut in spring:
Nani mo naki koso — There is nothing in it—
Nani mo are. — There is everything.

To the occidental mind, the sense of this famous haiku by Sodō (1641–1716) is elusive, if not outright contradictory. But to the oriental mind it is self-explanatory. This is so because the basic bias of Western philosophy and culture leans clearly in the direction of *being.* The good, the beautiful, and the creative are all defined in terms of being. Thus their imperfection or privation is considered a kind of *non-being.* The basic bias of the East, on the other hand, falls on *nothingness*—not the negative notion of the West, but a rich, all-encompassing void that is full of meaning and possibility. If the Western attraction to being finds its origins in ancient Greece, it is ancient India that can be called the philosophical cradle of the East. It is against this background that one must approach the reality of *mu*—that largely unconscious but terribly powerful idea at the root of so much of Japan's cultural psychology, a word for which we have no better term than "nothingness."

Related closely to the Buddhist notion of "emptiness" and its ideal of "selflessness," *mu-shin* (no-mind) is at the base of both the Japanese feeling of unity with all of nature and their calm resignation to fate. It looks for meanings in the empty spaces in paintings, in between the lines in literature, in the unspoken and unexplained aspects of communication. Similarly the spirit of *mu-i* (acting by letting go of action), is at work in such things as in the "effortless effort" of the judo master who uses the force of an attacker to overcome. Through mu-shin and mu-i, Japan succeeded in transforming the rubble of war into the wonders of industry and technology that characterize it today. Through mu-shin and mu-i Japan preserves the timelessness and effectiveness of its many arts and traditions. In short, mu and all its manifestations are to Japan what self-reliance, control, and stubborn perseverance are to

the West: largely unreflected frames of mind that seem to make sense only to those who live in them.

The famous story of the Chinese Zen Master Jōshū (778–897), who barked: *"Mu,"* in reply to the young monk's question of whether the dog has a Buddha-nature, well describes the kind of frustration the Westerner often feels in attempting to fathom the oriental mind. The problem, of course, comes with the kind of questions that seem perfectly logical to one party but beside the point to the other. Thus, only by achieving some appreciation of the power and reality of nothingness can the mysteries of the Japanese soul open up—and free the Westerner from the fetters of his own cultural prejudices.

Vladimir Devidé

Contributors

Barbara C. Adachi, American, born in China in 1924, spent her schoolgirl days in Japan, where she has lived since 1946. She studies, writes, and lectures in various fields of Japanese arts.

Harumi Befu, born in California in 1930, is a specialist in the study of social organization. At present he is a professor at Stanford University.

Frances Blakemore, born in America, is the author of *Japanese Design* and directs the Franell Gallery in Tokyo. Also an artist of wide repute, she has had a number of one-man shows.

Noah S. Brannen, born in Texas in 1924, has lived in Japan for twenty-eight years. At present he is a professor of linguistics, languages, and literature at International Christian University in Tokyo.

Holloway Brown, born in Virginia in 1919, has lived in Japan more than thirty years. At present he is an associate professor of journalism at International Christian University in Tokyo.

Jean-René Cholley, born in France in 1940, has been in Japan for thirteen years. At present he is an assistant professor in the foreign languages department of Aichi Prefectural University.

Gregory Clark, born in Australia in 1936, has experience as a diplomat and a journalist and is at present a professor at Sophia University in Tokyo. One of his books is *The Japanese Tribe.*

Thomas J. Cogan, born in Ohio in 1947, is at present a doctoral candidate at the University of Hawaii, where he studies Japanese literature.

William Currie, born in Philadelphia in 1935, specializes in comparative literature and is at present vice-president of Sophia University in Tokyo.

Rebecca M. Davis, American, first came to live in Japan in 1955, returning in 1971 to make her home in Tokyo, where she is a free-lance editor and book designer.

Vladimir Devidé, born in Zagreb in 1925, is at present a professor of mathematics at the University of Zagreb and a member of the Yugoslav Academy of Sciences and Arts.

Jean Esmein, born in France in 1923, has been an assistant professor at the University of Paris, press attaché at the French embassy in Peking, and also a banker in Japan, where he lived more than nine years and studied Japanese folklore.

Edward Fowler, born in America in 1947, is a specialist in Japanese literature. At present he is a doctoral candidate at the University of California.

Richard L. Gage, born in Virginia in 1934, has lived in Japan since 1964 and is a translator and editor.

Theodore Goossen, American, born in 1948, is at present a doctoral candidate at the University of Toronto, where he specializes in modern Japanese literature.

Lonny Joseph Gordon, born in Texas, is a solo concert artist and at present chairman of the department of modern dance technique at the University of Wisconsin. He has a great interest in Japanese classic dance.

Ruben Habito, Filipino, born in 1947, studied Buddhism at the University of Tokyo. At present he is a lecturer at Sophia University in Tokyo.

Thomas W. Hare, born in Colorado in 1952, is a doctoral candidate at the University of Michigan, where he studies Japanese literature.

Thomas J. Harper, born in America in 1939, obtained a doctorate with a thesis on *The Tale of Genji.* At present he is a senior instructor in the department of Japanese at the Australian National University.

James W. Heisig, born in Boston in 1944, specializes in the philosophy of religion and is at present an assistant professor at the Institute for Religion and Culture at Nanzan University in Nagoya.

Johannes Hirschmeier, born in Silesia in 1921, studied economics at Harvard University. He began teaching at Nanzan University in Nagoya in 1960 and is at present president of that university.

Gaynor Jenke, born in Australia in 1947, studied Japanese language and history at the Australian National University and is studying Buddhism in Japan.

Donald Keene, born in New York in 1922, is a well-known author and translator. In addition to his many other books, he has recently published the first thorough English-language history of Japanese literature. At present he is a professor at Columbia University.

Don Kenny, born in Kansas in 1936, has been in Japan since 1959. Fascinated with *Kyōgen,* he formed a troupe of players and has given several public performances in the United States.

Joseph S. Lapenta, born in New York in 1941, is an adept in *ikebana,* in which he holds a teacher's license. At present he works with Time-Life Educational Systems as an English instructor.

Trevor P. Leggett, born in London in 1914, long worked as head of the BBC Japanese service. At present he writes on judo, Zen, and so forth. He holds a sixth *dan* in judo (which is one of the higher ranks).

Edward J. Licht, born in Michigan in 1955, specialized in theater at Boston University. He came to Japan after graduation and is studying and practicing *Kyōgen.*

Anthony V. Liman, Canadian, born in 1932, specializes in modern Japanese literature. At present he is a professor at the University of Toronto.

Ruth Linhart, born in Austria in 1945, is a free-lance journalist and translator. She has translated Endō Shūsaku's *Chinmoku* (Silence) into German.

Sepp Linhart, born in Austria in 1944, specializes in Japanology and sociology. At present he is a professor and the president of the Institute of Japanology at the University of Vienna.

Karl Manougian, American, born in 1944, divides his time among New York, Rome, and Japan as a free-lance writer and simultaneous interpreter.

Patricia H. Massy, born in Florida, specializes in the study of Japanese traditional arts, in particular crafts and textiles. Living in Japan since 1966, she works as a free-lance writer.

Stephen W. McCallion, born in Pennsylvania in 1948, is a doctoral candidate at Ohio State University, where he majors in Japanese history, especially the period of the Meiji Restoration of 1868.

Peter Milward, born in London in 1925, is a specialist in the works of Shakespeare. He has lived in Japan since 1954 and is at present a professor of English literature at Sophia University in Tokyo.

Françoise Moréchand, born in Paris, majored in Japanology at the University of Paris, Sorbonne. At present director of the Moréchand Stylist Academy in Japan, she has written several books on fashion.

Wayne Murphy, born in Canada in 1950, studied the political history of the Meiji era at Keiō University and at present works as an English consultant.

Patricia Murray, born in Massachusetts in 1940, is executive editor of *The Japan Interpreter* and studies anthropology, particularly folk religions and occupational groups.

Walter Nichols, American, born in 1919 in Tokyo, was once a cultural attaché at the American embassy in Japan. At present he is president of Nichols Enterprises, Inc.

Leonard C. Pronko, American, born in 1927 in the Philippines, is a professor of Romance languages and an associate in theater at Pomona College. He is versed in Kabuki and Japanese dance.

Sharon Ann Rhoads, born in Washington, D.C., in 1944, is a free-lance writer and translator. Having long lived in Japan, she now lives in New York.

Donald Richie, born in Ohio in 1924, is a well-known film critic and the author of many books on Japanese films, literature, and arts. He continues to live and write in Tokyo, where he has lived since 1954.

Paul Rietsch, born in France in 1912, has been in Japan since 1948 and has written many books on Japan. At present he is a professor at Sophia University in Tokyo.

Lynne E. Riggs, born in Pennsylvania in 1950, studied Japanology at the University of Hawaii and is now working as a translator and editor.

Robert Rolf, born in Ohio, is now working on translations of *shingeki* plays. He lives in Fukuoka and teaches at Fukuoka University of Education.

Murray Sayle, Australian, has traveled worldwide as a journalist. At present he is a free-lance writer and lives in Japan.

Susan Schmidt, born in Illinois in 1946, specializes in political science and is an editor at the University of Tokyo Press.

Edward G. Seidensticker, born in America in 1921, is a well-known translator and scholar of Japanese literature and is renowned for his translation of *The Tale of Genji.* At present he is a professor at Columbia University.

John Stevens, born in Chicago in 1947, studied Zen and Buddhism and is a lecturer at Tōhoku College of Social Welfare. He is the author of *One Robe, One Bowl: The Zen Poetry of Ryōkan.*

Jan Swyngedouw, born in Belgium in 1935, has lived in Japan since 1961. At present he is an associate professor at the Institute for Religion and Culture at Nanzan University in Nagoya.

Richard F. Szippl, born in Ohio in 1951, is a graduate student in the department of theology at Nanzan University in Nagoya.

Alan Talbot, born in Australia, is at present a medical doctor at the hospital attached to Okayama University.

Jacques Thiriet, born in France in 1939, is a free-lance writer and has taught French in Japan for over ten years.

Suzanne Trumbull (Japanese name: Sōma Yuri), born in America, who has been in Japan for fifteen years and has recently acquired Japanese citizenship, is a director of and the head of the English-language department of Japan Echo Inc.

Beverley D. Tucker, American, born in 1925, is a professor in the department of English literature at Doshisha University in Kyoto and has written many articles on Japan.

Čiháková Vlasta, born in Czechoslovakia in 1944, has been in Japan for over ten years. At present she is a free-lance art critic.

Jeremy Whipple, born in Massachusetts in 1950, majored in linguistics and Japanese at Harvard University and at present works for the Dai-ichi Mutual Life Insurance Co. in Tokyo.

Richard Wood, born in Michigan in 1937, is at present chairman of the department of philosophy at Earlham College and specializes in modern Japanese philosophy.

Helen Yeung, born in China in 1955, majored in linguistics at International Christian University in Tokyo and is continuing her studies in Hong Kong.

The Historical Periods of Japan

Nara period	710–794
Heian period	794–1185
Kamakura period	1185–1336
Muromachi period	1336–1568
Momoyama period	1568–1603
Edo period	1603–1868
Modern period	
Meiji era	1868–1912
Taishō era	1912–1926
Shōwa era	1926–

Index

196	Ise	A famous Shinto pilgrimage site
80	Jieitai	The national defense forces
118	Jikatabi	Workmen's rubber-soled footwear
170	Jūdō	The sport of judo
84	Juku	Private supplementary schools
158	Kabuki	Kabuki theater
124	Kagi	Lock and key
46	Kaisō	Algae; seaweed
90	Kamon	Family crests
168	Kangeiko	Midwinter training for those in the martial arts
184	Kanji	The Chinese ideograms used in writing Japanese
188	Kappa	A mythical water imp
130	Kigumi	Wood joinery
180	Kinen-shashin	Commemorative photographs and snapshots
128	Kō	Incense
88	Koseki	The official family register
154	Kyōgen	Comic theatrical skits
174	Mājan	Mah-jongg
54	Makudonarudo	McDonald's restaurant-chain
60	Manaita	The cutting board
98	Minoue Sōdan	Personal advice
34	Miyamairi	The first visit of a baby to its tutelary shrine
14	Mizu	Water
206	Mu	Nothingness
126	Mushi-kago	Insect cages
164	Naniwabushi	A kind of chanted ballad
160	Nihonbuyō	Japanese dance
136	Nihontō	The Japanese sword
152	Nō	Nō drama
78	Nōkyō	Agricultural cooperatives
134	Noshi	Gift decorations
92	Ofukuro	Mom; Ma
200	O-henro	Pilgrimages
56	Okosama-ranchi	A special children's lunch
122	Okujō	Rooftops
86	Omawari-san	The patrolman
108	Onsen	Hot springs

106	O-seibo	Year-end gifts
64	Oshibori	A dampened towel served for one's refreshment
166	Piano	The piano
24	Rajio-taisō	Radio calisthenics
204	Rokudōsen	Coins to pay one's passage into the next world
114	Seifuku	Uniforms
94	Senpai	One's senior in school or at work
138	Sensu	The folding fan
148	Shakuhachi	A vertical bamboo flute
76	Shataku	Company housing
176	Shinbun	Newspapers
162	Shingeki	A twentieth-century theatrical form
20	Shinkansen	The superexpress bullet train
42	Shio	Salt
40	Shiwasu	The end-of-the-year rush
62	Shokuhin Sanpuru	Model food, displayed by restaurants
72	Shōsha	General trading companies
110	Shūgaku-ryokō	School excursions
116	Surippa	House slippers
30	Taifū	Typhoon
150	Taiko	The Japanese drum
190	Tanuki	The raccoon-dog
112	Tebukuro	Gloves
146	Teien	Landscape gardens
82	Tōdai	Tokyo University
16	Tsumikusa	Herb gathering
22	Tsuyu	The rainy season
44	Umeboshi	Pickled plums
32	Undōkai	A game and exercise meet
144	Urushi	Lacquer ware
132	Washi	Japanese paper
50	Yakumi	Condiments
66	Yatai	Movable stalls selling food and drink
120	Yojōhan	A four-and-a-half-mat room
96	Yopparai	Inebriation
38	Yukimizake	Drinking saké while enjoying the snow
198	Zazen	Zen meditation